Schumacher Briefing No. 4

THE ECOLOGY OF MONEY

Richard Douthwaite

published by Green Books
for The Schumacher Society

First published in 1999
by Green Books Ltd
Foxhole, Dartington, Totnes,
Devon TQ9 6EB
www.greenbooks.co.uk
greenbooks@gn.apc.org

for The Schumacher Society
The CREATE Centre, Smeaton Road,
Bristol BS1 6XN
www.oneworld.org/schumachersoc
schumacher@gn.apc.org

Cover design by Rick Lawrence

Printed by J.W. Arrowsmith Ltd
Bristol, UK

A catalogue record for this publication is available
from the British Library

ISBN 1 870098 81 1

CONTENTS

Foreword

by Bernard Lietaer

Four main benefits can be derived from reading Douthwaite's *Ecology of Money*:

1. He introduces much needed clarity in the domain of money. I like the simplicity of the six questions he uses to walk us through different money systems, a process which facilitates comparisons of the nature, advantages and disadvantages of each money system he describes.

2. He explores these different money systems using a terminology that lay people can understand. This is no minor achievement, as illustrated by economist John Kenneth Galbraith's quip that "The study of money, above all fields in economics, is the one in which complexity is used to disguise truth, or evade truth, not to reveal it." [1]

3. He forces us to think the unthinkable—the possibility that our familiar national currencies may actually be out-of-date in an age of globalization, information revolutions and planetary ecological hazards.

4. He presents some ideas for new money systems designed to help us with some of our biggest challenges of today.

In particular, two issues he addresses are highly relevant at this time:

• The need for a new balance between the global and the local economies; and

• The issue of carbon-energy efficiency.

Talking about small-scale local currencies in the middle of all the media buzz about globalization may sound parochial or marginal to some. It is not. Community rebuilding is not a contradiction with the trend towards a global civilization, but a necessary complement to it. Precisely because of the globalization trend, strengthening local community is becoming more important. Rather than argue from theory, I will contribute two case studies from Japan, clearly a globally oriented economy.

Japan has decided to introduce local currencies, complementary to the conventional national currency, to tackle two key problems which the West will be facing acutely soon—ageing populations and the need for new regional development strategies. Both examples illustrate Douthwaite's points.

Japan has one of the fastest ageing populations of the developed world. By the year 2005, the population over 65 years of age will reach 18.5% of the total (a situation that Germany will face by 2006, and the UK and France by 2016.)

A special currency called Hureai Kippu (literally 'Caring Relationship Tickets') has been created by a group of 300 non-profit organizations. The unit of account is an hour of service. The people providing the services can accumulate the credits in a 'healthcare time savings account' from which they may draw when they need credits for themselves, for example if they get sick. These credits complement the normal healthcare insurance program payable in Yen, the conventional Japanese national currency. In addition, many prefer to transfer part or all of their Hureai Kippu credits to their parents who may live in another part of the country. Two private electronic clearing houses have sprung up to perform such transfers. One particularly important finding has emerged. Because they have experienced a higher quality of care in their relationships with caregivers, the elderly tend to prefer the services provided by people paid in Hureai Kippu over those paid with the conventional Yen.

The second application is potentially even more impressive. The Ministry of International Trade and Industry in Japan (MITI) has recently concluded that the future of Japan's development strategy will be based on 'Silicon Valley'-type specialized regional economies, and that the best tool to stimulate such regional development clusters are local 'eco-money' systems. Four pilot projects have already tested this approach, and the results are convincing to the point that by end 1999 no less than forty such systems will be launched. Some of Japan's largest corporations (such as NTT and Oracle Japan) are involved in these experiments.

The point about these two examples is that theory is way behind practice in this domain. People are innovating in the monetary domain, and are obtaining demonstrably positive results from it, while the majority of the policy makers remain still unaware about the potential of monetary inventions to solve their problems. I would compare today's non-conventional money domain to aeronautics when the Wright Brothers took their first flights. The first airplane builders didn't know why their contraptions were flying, but fly they did. And it took the *New York Times* more than four years to even mention the event (and then only because the President of the US was witnessing a demonstration). Nevertheless, nobody questions that the aeronautical industry has changed forever our way of life on this planet.

Do I agree with all the ideas that are presented here? Even Douthwaite admits that he doesn't "expect everyone to agree with the conclusions he has reached".

For instance, although I agree with him on the importance of linking monetary issues to energy sustainability, I question the viability of the means he proposes. (Why not include his 'Energy-Backed Currency Units' (ebcu) as part of a basket of commodities and services backing the currency—rather than being the exclusive backing of currency? This would dampen the effects of price instabilities of the ebcu, due among other things to technological innovations in the supply of energy.)

I am also concerned about his benign view on inflation. Inflation has the positive effects Douthwaite mentions only if it occurs by surprise, i.e. has not been discounted by inflationary expectations. In other words, building inflation into the system may just kill whatever usefulness it has.

However these disagreements pale in comparison with my whole-hearted support of two of Douthwaite's key conclusions:

• Contrary to what most economists believe, money is not neutral, i.e. different money systems are now possible, and could make a dramatic difference in helping us with several of our most important challenges including ecological sustainability;

• "Only a widespread debate on the issues, by a well-informed public, will ensure that when changes are made [to the money system] they are along the right lines." To paraphrase the line about war and the military, money is too important to be left only to bankers and economists . . .

As the public is remarkably ill-informed about the nature of our money system, as even most experts seem to believe that there is no choice, starting a debate about the effects of different money systems on society is a vital task. In this sense, reading Douthwaite's contribution may be particularly useful because it is a controversial one.

Brussels
October 1999

Bernard Lietaer is a former Professor of International Finance at the University of Louvain in Belgium. He spent five years as head of the Organization and Planning Department at the Central Bank of Belgium where he was concerned with electronic payment systems and the design and implementation of the Ecu. He is currently developing inter-trading systems for community currencies. His book *The Future of Money* will be published by Random House in Spring 2000.

Glossary

Citizens' Income An income which, it is proposed, should be paid by the state to all citizens as a right, regardless of how much or how little they earn. It would replace income tax relief and social welfare payments.

Demurrage A fee charged for the use of a currency for a period of time. The fee is intended to encourage users to spend the money quickly, rather than hoarding it.

DTQs Domestic Tradable Quotas: a rationing device proposed by Dr. David Fleming to control emissions of CO_2. Both DTQ units and money would be needed to buy all types of energy. Each person would be allocated the same amount of DTQ units every month and, if they did not need them all, they would be able to sell the surplus to those who needed more.

ebcus Energy-Backed Currency Units. These would play the same role in the proposed international currency system that gold played in the days of the gold standard (*q.v.*). Their value in terms of SERs (*q.v.*) would be guaranteed by an international organization.

Fractional reserve banking Banking based on the practice of keeping reserves of cash worth only a fraction of the amount which customers would be entitled to withdraw if they chose to do so.

Gold standard The currency system under which the value of each national currency was related to a certain weight of gold, and thus to other national currencies.

Gold exchange standard A variant on the gold standard under which the US dollar was exchangeable for a fixed amount of gold, and all other participating currencies were exchangeable for US dollars.

LETS (Local Exchange Trading System) The acronym invented by Michael Linton for the local currency system he developed.

Scrip Privately printed paper money.

SERs (Special Emission Rights) The right to emit a specified amount of greenhouse gases and hence to burn fossil fuel.

Social Credit A body of ideas developed by C.H. Douglas between 1918 and 1922 which would, among other things, bring money creation under social control.

Stamped scrip Scrip (*q.v.*) to which a stamp had to be stuck at prescribed intervals to maintain its validity. The organizers of the currency collected a fee for supplying the stamps both to cover their operating costs and as a form of demurrage (*q.v.*).

Introduction & Summary

Most people think that there's only one type of money because one type is all they've ever known. They know about foreign currencies, but they see these, quite correctly, as essentially the same sort of money as they use in their own countries. They also know about cheques, credit and debit cards, credit notes, and several of the other forms that money can take but, correctly again, regard these simply as special-purpose versions of notes and coins. Money is money, they think, regardless of the form it takes. Only the few who know a little monetary history, or are members of a Local Exchange Trading System (LETS), realize that this is not the case. There are, potentially at least, many different types of money, and each type can affect the economy, human society and the natural environment in a different way.

Most economists think that there's only one type of money too. That is when they think about it at all. The profession, to quote two sociologists is "curiously uninterested [in the topic], restricting itself to discussions of price, scarcity and resource allocation with no specific interest in money as such."[1] David Hume, one of the founding fathers of economics, referred to money as "the oil which renders the motion of the wheels smooth and easy,"[2] and this attitude persists to this day. Indeed, Paul Samuelson's well-known economics textbook defines economics as "the study of how men and society choose, *with or without the use of money*, [my italics] to employ scarce productive resources".[3]

In other words, economists see money acting as a catalyst that eases and speeds up economic interactions that would have taken place anyway. Naturally, they are interested in the amount of money reaching circulation because that affects the pace at which the economy can run, and consequently determines whether national income rises or falls. However, very few seem to have ever considered the possibility that the particular type of monetary catalyst in use might be affecting the outcome of the economic interaction, and that if other forms of money were used the results might be quite different. The only economists even to glance in this direction are either Marxists or members of the Social Credit movement who, because of the nature of their beliefs, have cause to analyse and question the nature of money more closely than more typical members of their profession. The last big-name economists to concern themselves with different forms of money and their effects were Maynard Keynes,[4] Henry Simons and Irving Fisher in the 1930s, a period in which the money system was quite clearly dysfunctional.

This Briefing will show that history is littered with examples of monetary systems that operated on quite different lines to the one we know at present. If these systems had survived, they would have produced cultures most unlike today's unsustainable, unstable global monoculture. The Briefing will demonstrate that different money systems affect the world in different ways. Ecology is defined as 'the study of the set of relationships of a particular organism with its environment'.[5] Consequently, anyone who is unfazed by regarding money as an organism can consider this book an ecology of money. Some of the more enlightened economists will probably be happy to do so. Professor Paul Ormerod, whose books have done much to alert the public to the problems within his profession, writes that "conventional economics is mistaken when it views the economy and society as a machine whose behaviour, no matter how complicated, is ultimately predictable and controllable. On the contrary, human society is much more like a living organism—a living creature whose behaviour can only be understood by looking at the complex interactions of the individual parts."[6]

Certainly, if we wish to live more ecologically, it would make sense to adopt monetary systems that make it easier for us to do so. Note the plural here. It is not just a case of exchanging a monetary system that emerged as a result of a series of historical accidents for one to a conscious design. As each money system tends to lead to a particular set of consequences, we are likely to have to use three or four money systems simultaneously to produce the combination of characteristics that we want our society to possess.

Questions to ask

Young journalists are taught to ensure they answer six questions in every story they write: Who? What? When? Where? Why? and How?. This Briefing asks these same questions of every type of money discussed: commercially-produced money; people-produced money, and government-produced money.

1. Who issued the money? Was it the state, a financial institution, or the users of the money themselves?

2. Why did they do so? Was it as a method of taxation, to make a profit for their shareholders, or simply to provide the users with a means of exchange?

3. Where was the money created? Was it in the area where it was going to be used? Or was it elsewhere, with the result that would-be users had to sell goods or services outside their area to collect enough money to be able to trade among themselves?

4. What gives the money its value? Is it backed by gold or another commodity, a promise of some sort, or nothing at all?

5. How was the money created? Was it by people going into debt to a central organization? Or did the users simply agree to allow each other credit and generate it among themselves?

6. When was the money created? Was it done once, several times, or continuously as part of a system of creation and destruction that caters for people's trading needs?

We'll ask a seventh question too:

7. How well does (or did) it work? Economics textbooks state that money serves three main functions, so we need to assess a currency's performance in relation to them all. In other words, we should check how well each type of money serves as:

A. A medium of payment or exchange. A good payment medium makes it easy for people to buy and sell to each other. This means that it must be generally acceptable and have a high value for its weight so that it is easy to transfer from buyer to seller. It must also be divisible, so it can be used for small transactions as well as large ones. And, while there needs to be enough of it around to enable everyone who wants to buy or sell to be able to do so easily, there must be some limit on its availability so people keep their confidence in it and its acceptability is maintained.

B. A store of value. A currency is a good store of value if someone receiving it is able to use it to purchase the same amount of goods and services regardless of when they spend it—next month, next year, or when they retire.

C. A unit of account. Is the monetary unit a good one in which to keep financial records and to quote prices? Normally, people keep their accounts and quote prices in the currency they use most frequently, but in times of uncertainty, or high inflation, they may use another currency instead. During the German hyperinflation in the early 1920s, for example, shopkeepers quoted their prices and kept their records in US dollars although their customers were paying in marks.

There are circumstances in which these three roles can come into conflict with each other. When prices are falling rapidly, for example, the 'store of value' property of money becomes extremely attractive and people begin to hoard whatever money comes their way, in the knowledge that they will be able to buy more with it later on. This naturally interferes with the ability of the currency to act as an effective means of exchange. Shortages of money develop, and normal trading becomes difficult. In the 1930s, businesspeople even had to invent special currencies—the Swiss Wirtschaftsring (see Box 3 on pages 36-7) is a notable example—so that they could settle accounts among themselves. If, on the other hand, prices are soaring rather than falling, money becomes a poor store of value and holders rush to spend it as soon as they can. This leads to prices rising more rapidly still. In view of these conflicts, it seems doubtful whether countries that limit themselves to the use of just one form of money can expect all three functions of money to be adequately satisfied.

Plan of action

The first three chapters of this Briefing explain how the characteristics of money are determined by the way it is created and then put into circulation. Chapter One (Commercially-produced Money) explains that the commercial banks create almost all the money that we use and put it into circulation by allowing us to borrow it from them. It goes on to explore the consequences of this rather odd arrangement, among which are the present economic system's chronic instability and insatiable need for growth.

Chapter Two (People-produced Money) deals with the amazing monies that people have created to use among themselves. These include American tobacco warehouse receipts, inscribed clay tablets representing quantities of Egyptian wheat, and carved stones in the South Pacific that were too heavy for anyone to carry. Strings of seashells and today's LETS fall into this category too. The important feature about all these currencies is that they are only created when the society involved has resources, usually of human labour, which it wants to put to better use.

Chapter Three (Government-produced Money) shows how, down the centuries, this form of money has often caused serious inflation as it has been used as a system of tax collection. Henry VIII, for example, added large amounts of copper to the silver from which he made his coins so that he could make more of them. As a result, prices doubled and a rebellion broke out. Despite this ominous precedent, we discuss a current proposal that governments should create any additional money their countries need and spend it into circulation. If this system were introduced in Britain, it would allow tax cuts of around 16%.

Chapter Four (One Country, Four Currencies) attempts to weave all these threads together by devising a multi-level multi-currency system which would ease the world's transition to sustainability by improving the way in which the economy allocates scarce resources between the present and future generations. It proposes an international unit-of-account currency whose value would be based on the right to emit greenhouse gases. This would be linked, through a currency exchange market, to national currencies that were only used for trading and were not expected to hold their value over long periods of time. Special currencies would be launched to fulfil the store-of-value function. Lastly, local currencies would have a strong role to play as they would not only be used to overcome local shortages of national currency but also to raise funds for special purposes.

No consensus

The most important feature of this Briefing is its insistence on three things.

1. All monies should be created by, or on behalf of, their users, and not by institutions wishing to profit from the activity.

2. Different types of currency have to be used concurrently if the three key functions of money are to be adequately performed.

3. The international unit-of-account currency, to which all other monies would be related, has to represent, and thus protect, a truly scarce resource. In other words, when we save money, we should also be saving something vitally important, like the integrity of the natural world.

This Briefing is not, therefore, a judiciously balanced, middle-of-the-road report on some emerging consensus in the currency-reform area. Such a document would be impossible to write as, apart from the widespread and long-standing agreement that governments rather than banks should put money into circulation, monetary reformers don't seem to agree about anything. Instead, this Briefing is an attempt to discover why the present economic system breaks down catastrophically if economic growth fails to occur. It also suggests how the monetary system could be reformed to remove this defect, which obviously stands in the way of our achieving a sustainable world.

I don't expect everyone to agree with the conclusions I've reached. One friend, whose opinions I value, wrote: "This looks like being an extremely stimulating and thought-provoking Briefing." I understood this to mean "You've gone too far", particularly as his his letter went on: "You may be running a risk if you publish firm proposals, as presented in this draft, [as you may] find quite soon that you want to change them significantly." In other words, I'd gone much too far and might want to retreat. I've decided, however, to accept the risk of this happening and not to water things down. However, all the ideas I discuss are under development and if they change as a result of a debate provoked by this Briefing, their publication will have been worthwhile.

Readers should not feel that they need to understand every paragraph completely before moving on, though I hope that they will be able to do so. If, when they reach the end of the book, they accept the urgent need for a radical restructuring of the money-creation system and have some sort of feeling for the general direction the restructuring should take, that should be quite enough.

I greatly value the comments and suggestions received from those who read a draft of this paper. All of them gave considerable time and thought to their responses, which helped me to make significant improvements. In particular I want to thank: Alan Armstrong; James Bruges; David Fleming; Frances Hutchinson; Nadia Johanisova; Brian Leslie; Bernard Lietaer; Barbara Panvel (and her friends Bill, Andrew and Elizabeth); James Robertson; Emer O Siochru, and Alex Wilks. I would now welcome comments from other readers.

Richard Douthwaite
Cloona, Westport, Ireland
October 1999

Chapter 1

Commercially-produced Money

Let's start by asking the first of the questions identified in the Introduction about the type of money we know best: a typical national currency. Many people will be surprised that the answer to the first question 'Who creates it?', is not 'the government', nor 'the country's central bank', but 'the commercial banks'. Yet there is no conspiracy to hide this fact. In his well-known economics textbook, David Begg states: "Modern banks create money by granting overdraft facilities in excess of the[ir] cash reserves".[7] He adds: "Bank-created deposit money [the money that people can draw from their bank accounts] forms by far the most important component of the money supply in modern economies."

Dishonest goldsmiths

So how did money creation come to be privatized? This query takes us back to the late middle ages, when gold and silver coins were the main form of money. During this period, if anyone obtained a large amount of coins (more than they felt safe with) then they would deposit them with the local goldsmith, the only person in the area with a reliable strongroom or safe. The goldsmith would give a receipt in exchange. The oldest surviving British record of money being deposited with a goldsmith is dated 1633.[8] Initially, depositors called at the goldsmith to reclaim their coins whenever they wanted to make a payment, but as time went on some of them found it more convenient to transfer the goldsmiths' receipts instead. Thus, by 1670, receipts frequently had the words 'or bearer' on them as well as the depositor's name. As coins were heavy and risky to carry around, the new receipts quickly became the preferred method of settling bills.

Shortly afterwards, the goldsmiths would have noticed that they had many coins in their vaults which were never taken out. History doesn't record the name of the first goldsmith who was both smart and dishonest enough to realize that, as it was unlikely that all his customers would present receipts and demand their coins at once, he could make money by lending out a proportion of the coins entrusted to him and charging the borrowers interest on them. Indeed he might not actually have to part with any of the coins at all, because if he gave borrowers receipts with which to make their payments (instead of cash), it would be rare for those who had received the false receipts to bring them in and ask for real money. The only problem was to decide how many such receipts he could issue without being found out if receipt-bearers did actually want to collect coins in exchange. If several receipt-bearers came in a short period, and there wasn't enough gold and silver money in his safe to pay them, he'd be disgraced and forced out of business.

This piece of sharp practice by a long-dead goldsmith laid the foundations of modern fractional reserve banking—the system under which banks maintain reserves of coins and notes in their vaults worth only a fraction of the cash they would have to provide if all their customers came simultaneously to demand the money they were entitled to withdraw. The goldsmith had created purchasing power (in other words, money) by issuing receipts that, in total, involved him in promising to pay out more gold and silver money than he had in his safe. Modern banks create money in the same way, by promising to pay out more paper notes and coins than they possess.

How banks create money

Begg explains how modern banks create money in the following way. He assumes that there are ten banks, each trying to maintain its lending at the point at which the amount of cash held in reserve in its vaults, or with the central bank, is equal to 10% of the amount that its customers could draw out from their accounts. The total amount that account-holders could withdraw (in other words, the bank's liability to its customers) not only consists of their deposits, but also any loan and overdraft facilities that they may have been granted but which they have not yet drawn upon.

If one of the ten banks receives a lodgement of £100 in cash, both the amount of notes and coins it holds in its safe, and the total of its liabilities to its customers, rise by that amount. However, the bank's liability-to-cash-reserve ratio is no longer the 10:1 it wants to

Box 1: How the Bank of England controls the money supply

The explanation of the way banks create money makes it appear that the amount of notes and coins in circulation, coupled with the reserve ratio the banks set themselves, determine the extent of a country's money supply. Actually, this is not quite the case. In most countries, the central bank does not attempt to control the total value of the notes and coins in circulation. In Britain, for example, the Bank of England (BoE) will sell as many notes and coins to the commercial banks as they wish. It simply debits the accounts these banks operate with it by the appropriate amount. So the cash base of the British monetary system is not just the notes and coins that the banks have in their branches, but whatever money they have in their accounts with the BoE as well.

Another minor difference is that it is not the commercial banks themselves that decide the reserve ratio they want to follow, but the central bank to which they report. For example, in Britain until 1981, the BoE specified the total amount of notes and coins a bank must have available at its branches, plus the amount on deposit with it, in relation to the amount of money the bank had created by granting its customers overdrafts and other loans. This meant that if at any time the BoE felt that the amount of money in circulation was too high and was causing inflation, it could force banks to reduce their lending by requiring them to deposit more funds in their accounts. A reduction in the reserve ratio from 20:1 to 10:1 would have halved the total of the amount of money that banks could create.

That system still applies but in a less rigid form. Responding to pressure from the commercial banks (who argued that they would otherwise lose overseas business to foreign banks), the BoE abolished its minimum reserve ratio in 1981. It now agrees a reserve requirement individually with each bank. This reflects both the level of competition the bank is experiencing from its foreign rivals, and the lending and other risks that it is perceived to be running. This change has weakened the BoE's ability to control the money supply by varying the reserve ratio.

The second way that the BoE can control the money supply is by 'open market operations'. These involve the BoE in buying, or selling, interest-bearing bonds. If it sells bonds, the purchasers (financial institutions or members of the public), pay for them by writing out cheques drawn on their commercial bank accounts in favour of the BoE. Subsequently, the BoE debits the accounts that the commercial banks operate with it by the

(Box 1 continued) relevant amounts. Unless the commercial banks make up these debits in some way, the volume of lending they are able to make (and thus the amount of money in circulation), has to be reduced by a figure set by whatever the reserve ratio they had agreed with the central bank. If the ratio were 20:1, their lending would have to be reduced by twenty times the amount of bonds that the BoE had sold.

If the reserve requirement is increased, or the amount in its account with the BoE falls, a bank could maintain its lending by raising more capital and depositing this with the central bank. The new capital could come from selling more shares, or from making a trading profit and paying that to the BoE rather than distributing it to shareholders as a dividend. For many years the Irish commercial banks attempted to justify their huge profits with the argument that they were necessary to enable the banks to lend enough money to finance a rapid expansion of business activity. Profits made by the UK's twelve banks and former building societies quoted on the Stock Exchange are high too. In 1998/9 they totalled £22bn, around £400 for every man, woman and child in the country. If the BoE wants to increase the amount of money in circulation, it can do so by buying up bonds that it, or perhaps a local council, had issued previously.

The third way in which the BoE can control the national money supply is to alter the interest rate at which it lends funds to banks that fail to keep positive balances in their accounts with it. According to an official BoE statement,[9] this is the main way that the money supply is controlled at present. The technique involves keeping the banking system short of money and then lending the banks the money they need at an interest rate that the BoE decides. The BoE statement explains, "If, on a particular day, more funds move from the private sector [i.e. non-government accounts held in the commercial banks], to the Government's accounts than vice versa, for example because banks' customers are paying their taxes, then the banking system will be short of the funds needed [by the commercial] banks to maintain positive balances on their accounts at the Bank." Alternatively, if the government is spending more than it is collecting, the BoE can create a shortage by selling bonds itself. The Bank then lends the banks the funds they need to keep their accounts with it in credit at a rate of interest that sets the rates at which the banks lend to each other, and to their customers. And that rate of interest, of course, determines how much the banks' customers borrow, and hence the national money supply.

maintain. It has £90 too much cash and if it increased its liabilities by lending £900 to its customers, its desired ratio would be restored. But should it make the £900 loan? What would happen if the person granted the new overdraft drew all £900 out as cash and spent the money in businesses that deposited their takings in rival banks? In this case, the bank's liability-to-cash-reserve ratio would be greater than 10:1, and there would be a risk that the bank might be unable to cash its customers' cheques if an unusual number of them came at the same time—perhaps just before Christmas, when a lot of cash enters circulation.

The only safe course for the bank to take is to lend out £90 rather than £900. Then, if the entire amount gets withdrawn as cash and ends up in other banks, its cash reserve ratio will still remain within the desired limit. In his explanation Begg assumes that the £90 is withdrawn and spent in such a way that all ten banks have an equal amount (£9) deposited with them. He could have equally, and more plausibly, assumed that it ended up with the banks in proportion to their size. No matter, the outcome would have been the same. If each bank now lends out 90% of whatever deposit it has received, that will create further deposits throughout the banking system. And if 90% of that money is lent out too, through an infinite number of lending rounds, then the banking system as a whole (rather than the bank which received the initial deposit) will have generated £900 in loans. This occurs just on the basis of the original reserve surplus of £90 in cash. In other words, the original £100 cash deposit allows the ten banks to increase their loans to the public (and hence the money supply), by £1,000.

So the answer to question one, 'Who creates money?', is that almost all of it is created by commercial banks, although, as Box 1 (pages 18-19) explains, central banks limit the extent to which they are able to do so. Most people find this answer quite staggering. Even bankers do. Lord Stamp, a director of the Bank of England at the time, commented in 1937: "The modern banking system manufactures money out of nothing. The process is perhaps the most astounding piece of sleight of hand that was ever invented." As the economist J. K. Galbraith remarked: "The process by which banks create money is so simple the mind is repelled. Where something so important is involved, a deeper mystery seems only decent." [10]

Let's move on to our other questions:

Question 2: Why do commercial banks create money? To make profits.

Question 3: How do they create money? By granting loans on which interest is paid. This means that almost all the money in a country exists because someone, somewhere, has gone into debt and is paying interest on it.

Question 4: When do they create money? Whenever there is a demand for loans at interest rates above that at which they can borrow from the central bank.

Question 5: What gives the money its value? This hasn't been mentioned yet, but the answer is purely its acceptability to other people. The value is not guaranteed. No one is standing by prepared 'to supply a fixed amount of something tangible in exchange, as they were in the days when paper currency could be exchanged on demand for a definite weight of gold. The value of modern money is constantly eroded by inflation. It is backed by nothing at all.

Question 6: Where is the money created? In the banks' head offices, wherever those may be. For although decisions on individual loans are made in hundreds of bank branches around the country (and the book-keeping side of money creation is done there too), each branch works within limits and to policies set by its head office. The profits generated by the lending also flow to the head office. Places using bank-created money for trading locally can only obtain money if they are prepared to borrow it on the same terms as other bank customers, or if they can sell goods and services to the outside world to earn money that people in other communities have borrowed. The fact that there is a branch bank in the community means nothing.

A little more discussion is needed to answer the intriguing problems posed by Question 7, namely 'How well does this sort of money fulfil the three functions of money?' and 'What are the consequences of allowing commercial companies to create it in this peculiar way?' The first thing to note is that as bank-created money only exists because people have borrowed it, it will cease to exist if they pay their loans off. This is because when borrowers assemble the funds they need to repay their loans and lodge them with their banks, those funds cease to be available to other people to use for trading unless the bank lends them out again. The money supply therefore contracts. Consequently, people need to take out new loans to maintain the amount of money in circulation.

Circumstances could easily arise in which they would not be prepared to borrow more, and the economy could plunge into a depression. For example, suppose a crisis overseas caused exports to fall sharply. As redundancies at home increased and people lost their confidence about their future prospects, they might be unwilling to take out new loans. However, if they continued to meet the interest and capital payments due on their existing debts, thereby reducing the total sum they owed, then the amount of money in circulation in the country would fall. Unless 'the velocity of circulation' of money increased (in other words, money moved from account to account fast enough to compensate for the fact that there was less of it about), then the volume of buying and selling going on in the country would also fall. Indeed, this would be bound to happen at some point when the rise in the velocity of circulation of the money became unable to counteract the diminishing supply. There is nothing remotely contentious about this. After all, it is the reason why central banks put up the interest rates at which they lend to commercial banks at the first sign of inflationary pressure. By doing so borrowing is cut, the money supply is reduced (or at least its growth is moderated), and excessive demand is reduced.

Moreover, even if the velocity of circulation did increase to make up for the fall in the amount of money, the ability of businesses to make profits would be reduced. Profits are recorded by businesses that have more assets at the end of a year than at the beginning. These assets can either be goods (finished stock, work-in-progress, raw materials, capital equipment) or cash and accounts receivable. If the amount of money that businesses have in their bank accounts and on their premises falls because the money supply has been reduced, the value of their other assets has to increase by more than enough to offset these falls if profits are to be made. But if firms place tight limits on the amount of raw materials and finished goods they carry in stock, and on customer credit—steps they would automatically take when their bank accounts are low—they will find it impossible to make profits. Many businesses will start to run at a loss. As a result, few will carry out investment projects the following year. Instead, rather than expanding, firms are likely to attempt to restore their profits by reducing staff. Job losses will become widespread, not just in the companies that would have built and equipped the new developments had the investments gone ahead, but also in the firms that would have made the investments themselves.

Against this background, the public's aversion to further borrowing will grow, especially as, with reduced earnings, many people will be having problems servicing their existing loans. 'Neither a borrower nor lender be' will become a popular maxim again. Even those with money to spend won't rush to do so in view of the uncertainty of the times and the fact that, because firms in distress will be cutting their prices, anyone with money will be able to purchase whatever they need more cheaply later on. This reluctance to spend will slow the circulation of money, effectively reducing the money stock even more. A severe depression will develop, exactly as happened in the 1930s and for the very same reasons.

Fundamental problems

Creating money on the basis of debt, therefore, makes the economic system fundamentally unstable. The system is always balanced on a knife-edge. If bank customers borrow too little, the economy moves into recession and, unless corrective action is taken, the positive feedbacks just discussed (such as people's natural reluctance to borrow and spend) will kick in and produce a catastrophic depression. Indeed, the main reason that a serious depression has not developed in Western Europe and North America since the 1930s is that semi-automatic corrective mechanisms have been unwittingly incorporated into the system. One of these, unemployment pay (and the social welfare system generally), has been a particularly important means of preventing crashes. It has ensured that, whenever the rate of joblessness has increased, larger amounts of money have automatically been transferred to people who spent all of it immediately. This is a very effective way of compensating for the loss of spending power. Another corrective mechanism is that whenever the economy has turned down, many people and firms have been forced to increase their bank debts involuntarily, simply to survive. This has increased the money supply to everyone else. However, if an economic shock was sufficiently severe, these twin buffering mechanisms would be overwhelmed and a serious depression would develop.

Another fundamental problem with the debt method of creating money is that, because interest has to be paid on almost all of it, the economy must grow continuously if it is not to collapse. Perhaps the best way of explaining this is to use the question asked when gold was the main currency. Since the gold being borrowed did not increase itself and very little was being mined, where was the extra amount of gold to come from to pay the interest when both principal and interest had to be paid at the end of the year? Obviously, as borrowers could only obtain the extra gold they needed by bringing about situations in which others had less, lending money at interest necessarily meant that borrowers either had less gold themselves after paying interest, or that they had impoverished someone else. As either outcome was socially undesirable, both the Roman Catholic Church and Islam condemned usury—all forms of money lending at interest, no matter how low the interest rate—as immoral.

Just because we now use paper currencies doesn't mean that the problem of 'where is the interest to come from?' has disappeared. Borrowers can only obtain enough money to pay their interest bills without reducing the amount of money in circulation if they, or other borrowers, borrow an adequate amount more. As a result, under the current money creation system, the amount of money in circulation has to rise, year after year, by a sum at least equivalent to the amount being removed from circulation by the banks as a result of interest payments. The amount removed is equal to the profits left to the banks after they have paid dividends to their shareholders in the country concerned, invested in new equipment and premises, and met all their wages, salaries and other operating costs there. These profits will be held in accounts in the banks' own names and unless they are put back into circulation by being spent or lent, the amount of money in circulation will fall. As a result, the business sector will show a loss and cut back its investment and borrowing, thus pushing the whole economic system into decline. The only thing to prevent this from happening would be that, by chance, the country's foreign earnings or capital inflow rose by enough to compensate for the interest lost.

The fact that the amount of money in circulation usually has to increase each year to enable interest to be paid means that the total value of sales in the economy has to go up too if the ratio of the money supply (and thus debt) to the volume of trading is to stay constant. The required increase in sales value can come about in either, or both, of two ways: inflation and expansion. If there is no increase in output during the year, the increased amount of money in circulation could simply push up prices, or allow firms to increase them. This inflation would provide businesses with enough additional income to pay their increased interest bills. The alternative is that the output of the economy grows by enough to require the monetary increase. This is the expansion. Of course the most likely outcome is a combination of inflation and expansion which will restore the balance between the value of trading and the value of money.

This analysis means that, due to the way money is put into circulation, we have an economic system that needs to grow or inflate constantly. This is a major cause of our system's continuous and insatiable need for economic growth, a need that must be satisfied regardless of whether the growth is proving beneficial. If ever growth fails to materialize, and inflation does not occur, the money supply will contract and the economy will move into recession. Politicians naturally do not want inflations and recessions occurring during their periods in office, so they work very closely with the business community to ensure that growth takes place. This is despite the damage that continual expansion is doing, both to human society and the natural world.

The impossibility of perpetual growth
Continuous economic growth is impossible in a finite world. True, some people believe that growth can be made environmentally harmless ('angelized', to use Herman Daly's term) by being stripped of its energy and natural resource content, so that it is capable of being continued indefinitely. But this is a pipe dream. The energy and resource content of many activities can certainly be reduced so that we can do more of them without increasing our environmental impact, but that impact cannot be reduced to nothing. Sooner or later, angelizing efforts will reach a point at which the amount of energy and other resources saved by further improvements in technology have become minimal. This will make further significant

increases in the volume of production impossible without causing additional environmental damage.

So could growth continue endlessly if it was the value of production which increased, rather than its physical volume? Technological optimists suggest that people might be prepared to pay more for goods and services of superior design or performance but the same resource content. However, even moving everything up-market has its limits. After a time, consumers would become unhappy paying extra for increasingly minor improvements.

No part of the economy has been angelized already, not even parts of the service sector. Indeed, once the inputs required (vehicles, buildings, copying machines) are taken into account, this sector might not be much less environmentally harmful than many industrial activities.

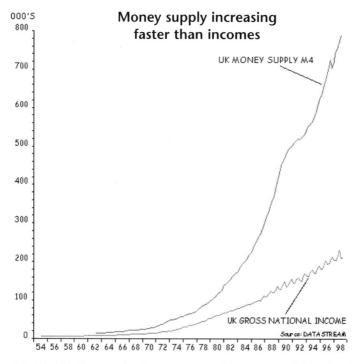

Money supply increasing faster than incomes

Britain's M4, the supply of money created by commercial banks plus the amount of notes and coins in circulation, has grown by twice as much as the country's national income since the early 1980s. The only part of its money supply on which no interest is paid, the notes and coins, has fallen from 7.4% to 3.6% of the total supply in the same period.

"That most services require a substantial physical base is evident from casual observation of a university, a hospital, an insurance company, a barber shop, or even a symphony orchestra," Daly says.[11] In any case, who would want angelized growth if it was not required to keep the economic system from breaking down? It would certainly do nothing for the poor, as Daly points out: "If the . . . expansion is really going to be for the sake of the poor,

A good store of value?

Britain's consumer prices
Jan 1974=100

Source: ONS

British consumer prices have gone up by over 600% since 1974.

then it will have to consist of things needed by the poor—food, clothing, shelter—not information services. Basic goods have an irreducible physical dimension." [12]

The fact is that, if we want to build a sustainable economic system—one that has the potential to continue unchanged for hundreds of years, without consuming the social and environmental resources it needs to operate—we have to give high priority to scrapping a money supply system that collapses if it is denied continuous expansion and not permitted to inflate. Sustainability requires a money supply system that can run satisfactorily if growth stops. Consequently, we need to add an eighth question to our list: 'Is this money supply system compatible with the achievement of sustainability?'

We can now sum up the performance of the present dominant form of money by answering the last two questions:

Question 7: How well does bank-created money work?

A: As a means of exchange? Since the end of the First World War, it has been extremely rare to have long periods in which the supply of money has been just right for the volume of trading. Either too much money got into circulation and inflation threatened, or too little, resulting in recessions or even a depression. Governments and central banks have devoted a great deal of effort to trimming the monetary controls and, because of the long response times before the

Fluctuations of the Dollar against the Pound

The exchange rate of the dollar in terms of sterling is now so unstable that it is of little use in planning for the future.

results of their adjustments appeared, they were very likely to overcorrect. A money supply system should be fundamentally stable rather than fundamentally unstable, as this one is.

B: As a store of value? Since 1918, most of the attempts to control the money supply have been intended to enable the monetary unit to serve as a reasonable store of value by preventing, or rolling back, inflation. These efforts were not notably successful and resulted in frequent large fluctuations in the value of one national currency in relation to another, often within the space of a few weeks. The record is poor even in terms of what a currency unit could buy within its national borders. The best that money-holders have come to expect within the past decade has been a loss of purchasing power of 3-4% a year. The reason for this gentle (but appreciable) decline is that monetary functions A and B conflict. Thus, if a central bank ever ensures that the store of value function is maintained perfectly, too little money gets into circulation to provide easy trading conditions. This causes profits to decline, investment to fall and the rate of unemployment to rise. Monetary supply management is therefore reduced to securing the least-bad compromise between two incompatible objectives.

C: As a unit of account? The record here is poor in two respects. One is that, because inflation has had to be allowed to take place continually to enable there to be adequate supplies of the means of exchange, it is difficult to make meaningful comparisons between financial results several years apart. The usual method is to convert them all to a common unit (1990 pounds, for example). These conversions are not always simple to make because the prices of various components of output, or cost, will almost certainly have changed by different percentage amounts. Even comparing one year's results with the next can be misleading. As a result, retail businesses' annual reports frequently correct a year's sales figures for price changes before comparing them with those of the previous year.

A more fundamental, and serious, problem with the use of modern money as a unit of account is that, as its value has no fixed, guaranteed relationship to anything tangible, it can lead to a gross misuse of resources. Cost-benefit analysis—a technique widely used to compare alternative ways of achieving the same objective over a period of time—shows this well. Suppose the objective is to meet an increasing demand for electricity. For instance, in Finland in 1999 two alternative ways of meeting an increased demand for electricity were being compared. The first was to build another nuclear power plant. The second was to employ people to turn the waste wood left in the forest after timber extraction into wood chips to be burnt in combined heat and power plants.

The costs and benefits of these alternative solutions naturally occur at different times in the future. For example, the nuclear plant would require very heavy spending in the ten years of construction. For 30 years after that, however, the operating costs would be very low and the benefits, in terms of the power produced, high. But after closure, the benefits would stop while the costs of dismantling would continue for over a hundred years and the costs of safe waste storage

For most of the 42-year period between 1935 and 1977, anyone hoping that investing in shares would enable their savings to keep pace with inflation was likely to have been disappointed.

for centuries. The wood waste alternative would involve less capital investment and give a more rapid start to the flow of benefits, but because of the wages of the workers involved, it would have much higher annual operating costs for as long as power was produced.

Analysts attempt to compare such projects by calculating for each cost and benefit the sum of money which, if invested today, would grow to be equivalent to the estimated amount of the cost or benefit in the year in which it occurs. These sums are known as the 'present values' of the benefits or costs. The analysts add up all the present values of the costs of a project and deduct them from the total of the present values of all the benefits. The project that has the greatest surplus of benefits over costs is the one they recommend for adoption.

The interest rate at which the money invested today is assumed to be able to grow is obviously crucial to the outcome of these calculations. Many firms use a rate of 10%, which means that a benefit of £10 million in 25 years' time has a present value of only £1 million today, while £10 million in year fifty is worth only £100,000. In other words, at such an interest rate, the costs of dismantling the nuclear station and storing its waste indefinitely have almost no impact on the result of the calculation. So projects that deliver their benefits soon and their costs far into the future always win. The mathematician, Colin Clark, was able to show this in a famous article.[13] He worked out that it was economically preferable to kill every blue whale left in the ocean as fast as possible, rather than to wait until the population of the species had recovered to the point at which it could sustain an annual catch. With the nuclear power example, it is even conceivable that dismantling the station and disposing of its waste might consume more energy than the plant gave out during its operating life, but that a cost-benefit analysis wouldn't reveal this.

That's why we need a money that acts as a proper unit of account. Present value calculations are only possible because our money means nothing. If, instead of pounds sterling, the unit of account for long-period calculations represented kilowatt-hours of electricity or even blue whales, people doing cost-benefit analyses would not be able to blithely reduce the value of costs and benefits arising years in the future in the cavalier way they do. To be a satisfactory unit of account, a money has therefore to represent something of real and lasting value. Its value cannot be set, as is modern money's, on an

Box 2: Why does our present money system lead to a long-term misuse of resources?

Because of the type of money we use at present, the prices set by the market at any given moment have nothing to do with long-term values. They are therefore entirely inadequate for determining the development path that we should select. The problem arises because the market is a human construct that works according to rules people have devised for it. Currently, those rules prevent millions of people without money from affecting the price levels in the market. The needs of the unborn cannot be expressed in the market either. Consequently, the prices that emerge from the market merely reflect the immediate wants of that fraction of the world's present population fortunate enough to have the money to be able to express them.

The ideal use of resources over the years can only be assessed in terms of one's objectives. At present, the system's objective is simply to minimize costs from moment to moment in terms of market prices that are largely determined by the current pattern of income distribution. This inevitably leads to a gross misallocation of resources in favour of the present. A key step toward sustainability is therefore to establish a unit-of-account currency which represents absolute amounts of something important to the whole world's population, present and future, rather than current transitory price levels determined by a temporary minority.

infinitely compressible scale. The values that a good unit-of-account currency might represent are discussed in Chapter 4.

Question 8: Is the money supply system compatible with sustainability? No, because it requires the value of production to rise constantly if the ratio of debt to output is not to build up and create loan-servicing difficulties, which might possibly tip the economy into depression. Only economic growth can maintain the debt-to-output ratio on a permanent basis, while simultaneously allowing investment to continue, and thus avoid the crisis that would follow if investment stopped. However, as we discussed, continuous growth is incompatible with a sustainable world.

A second reason for regarding the current money supply system as a barrier to sustainability is that, as it is an inadequate unit of account, it is difficult, if not impossible, for the economic system to allocate resources properly between present and future uses.

The problems with the present system of money creation can be summarized as follows:

1. The system creates a highly unstable economic climate.

2. The system requires continual economic growth if it is not to collapse. It is therefore incompatible with sustainability.

3. The system is pre-disposed to competition rather than co-operation as, with a limited amount of money in circulation, people and firms have to compete for it in order to survive.

4. The system's money is created outside the communities in which it is used. So money has either to be earned by the export of goods and services from those communities, or borrowed by them. This undermines local self-reliance.

5. The money supplied by the system is not created by the users as, and when, it is needed. Instead, it is created for them by profit-seeking organizations whenever the central bank thinks that inflation is under control. Shortages that prevent people meeting their needs can therefore arise.

6. The money created by the commercial banks does not represent anything real. Thus, an economic system based on its use is an ineffective way of allocating resources in short supply between current uses and those likely to arise in the future. A money system should be developed that represents the world's most critical scarce resource at the present time. People's natural, and constant, efforts to save money would then automatically involve them in saving the resource.

Chapter 2

People-produced Money

If an economic system is to move towards sustainability, and to maintain it once it has been achieved, it needs to establish what is the scarce resource whose use it seeks to minimize. Systems and technologies can then be adjusted to bring the least-use solution about. Unfortunately, the present economic system regards money as the scarce resource when, as we have seen, it can be created at will by a few account entries. The idea that money is the scarce resource is a relic from the days when money consisted of gold and silver coins. At that time, the world was essentially on an energy standard, because the amount of gold produced in a year was determined by the cost of the energy it took to extract it. If energy (perhaps in the form of slave labour rather than fossil fuel) was cheap and abundant, gold mining would prove profitable, and a lot of gold would go into circulation, enabling the economy to expand. If the increased level of activity then drove energy prices up, the flow of gold would decline, slowing the rate at which the economy grew.

Gold was often a people-produced form of money, rather than a governmental or commercially generated one. Theoretically, it was possible for anyone to pan for it in a stream or sort through a bed of gravel containing nuggets, thus converting their time and energy, plus some bought-in supplies, into something exchangeable for goods and services all over the world. Gold rushes were all about the conversion of human energy into money. They were, and are—as the thousands of ordinary people mining in the Amazon basin show—a democratic form of money creation. Obviously if supplies of food, clothing and shelter were precarious, people would never devote their energies to finding something that they could neither eat, nor live in, and which would not keep them warm. In other words, gold supplies swelled whenever a culture was producing a surplus. Once there was more gold about, the use of the precious metal as money made more trading possible and thus catalysed the conversion of whatever surpluses arose in future years into buildings, clothes and other needs.

There are plenty of historical accounts of this type of conversion. Before transport systems improved and money became widely available, rural people in many parts of the world had a potential surplus in the form of spare time. They could have easily increased their agricultural, construction or craft output, but didn't do so as there wasn't a market for the extra produce. Instead, they spent some of their surplus by helping their neighbours through mutual-aid systems that they used like banks, confident that they would be repaid. "The giver, by giving, guaranteed that he would be the receiver in the future," Hugh Brodie writes in his study of Irish rural life.[14] He continues: "In that way, the giving of surplus to friends and neighbours is not very far from the giving of surplus to the cashier in a bank. The quality of integrated society, like the legal rules of banking, guaranteed that the gift would not be forgotten and a future claim ignored." But when money became available and the surplus could be converted to it, people saved actual cash for a rainy day rather than storing up favours with their neighbours.

Creating currencies from unused resources

Rather than converting a surplus into gold to use as money, the inhabitants of a group of islands in the Pacific Ocean converted theirs into carved stones to use as currency. According to Glyn Davies' mammoth study, *The History of Money*:[15]

The peculiar stone currency of Yap, a cluster of ten small islands in the Caroline group of the central Pacific, was still used as money as recently as the mid-1960s. The stones known as 'fei' were quarried from Palau, some 260 miles away, or even the more distant Guam, and were shaped into discs varying from saucer sized to veritable millstones, the larger specimens having holes in the centre through which poles could be pushed to help transport them. Despite centuries of at first sporadic, and later more permanent, trade contacts with the Portuguese, Spanish, German, British, Japanese and Americans, the stone currency retained and even increased its value, particularly as a store of wealth.

Davies adds that shell necklaces, individual pearl shells, mats and ginger supplemented the stone currency, but he quotes from a book published in 1952, when fei were still in use, to the effect that the stones were "the be-all and end-all of the Yap islander. They are not only money, they are badges of rank and prestige, and they also have religious and ceremonial significance."[16]

It is often said that gold makes a good currency because of its 'intrinsic value', but this is nonsense. Gold is no more or less intrinsically valuable than hundreds of other commodities. True, it is an attractive metal that doesn't tarnish, but satisfactory substitutes can be found for most of its uses. Fundamentally, it has no greater intrinsic value than did the Yap islanders' stones or any of the other many things that people have used as a base for their money systems. These have included salt, silk, dried fish, feathers, stones, cowrie shells, beads, cigarettes, cognac and whisky, and livestock. The word 'pecuniary' comes from *pecunia*, the Latin for cow; and 'fee' is a corruption of the German word *Vieh*, meaning cattle. In 1715, the government of North Carolina declared seventeen commodities, including maize and wheat, to be legal tender.

In ancient Egypt, grain was the monetary unit. The farmers would deposit their crops in government-run warehouses in return for receipts showing the amount, quality and date. These stores suited the farmers because they protected the grain against theft, fire and flood, and also saved them the cost of providing their own storage facilities or selling their crop immediately after harvest when prices were low. The stores also enabled them to pay their rent and to buy goods simply by writing what was effectively a cheque, to transfer grain from their account in the store to that of someone else. People using another grain store in another part of the country could be paid with these cheques. The various stores would balance out their claims against each other just as banks do today. This meant that the grain would only be moved if there was a net flow of cheques from one area to another and if it was actually needed there for consumption. In other words, the weight of corn was merely a basis for accounting and the corn itself was not a standard barter good.

Tobacco stores in the New England states operated in much the same manner and enabled the crop to serve as legal tender in Virginia and Maryland for almost two hundred years. As Galbraith points out,[17] this was longer than the gold standard managed to survive. An important feature of both grain and tobacco as currencies was that whoever made a deposit was not only charged for keeping

Box 3: Businesses organize their own currency to overcome money drought

One way that businesses can continue to make profits in periods in which the supply of national currency is inadequate is to allow each other credit. As discussed in Chapter One, the credit-control measures that most firms use to protect themselves whenever trading becomes difficult actually make matters worse. While it would obviously be a mistake for firms to have no credit control at all, what businesses need when national currency becomes scarce is a properly regulated system of mutual credit so that they can use much less normal money when they trade amongst themselves. The Swiss Wirtschaftsring (Economic Circle) co-operative (WIR) is such a system. It was launched in 1934 by a group of businesspeople to overcome the currency shortages of the time and has since grown into a massive organization. In 1993, its 60,000 account holders turned over 2,521 million Swiss francs (£1,200 million).

The founders' idea was simply that traders who knew and trusted each other would extend credit for purchases within their group, cutting down their need to borrow from banks. According to report on the system in 1971, "they thought they could transact business among themselves with a system of chits similar to IOUs that would cover at least part of the price of any transaction, the balance being settled in the conventional way. (However) it was soon found that in order to bring about wider acceptance of these chits, and also to comply with existing banking laws and avoid financial losses, collateral was essential."

This insistence on collateral might partially explain why WIR has survived and similar systems established at the same time in other countries have disappeared without trace. However, an official history of WIR[18] produced for its 50th anniversary suggests that WIR is the sole survivor because the other systems did not realize the significance of what they were doing and closed down after the financial crisis was past. But opposition from vested interests played a part in some cases too. The founders visited circles in Norway and Denmark before starting WIR, and when they returned to Denmark for a second visit, they found that the government had closed the circle there after pressure from the banks.

Essentially, WIR is an independent currency system for small and medium-sized businesses. A company wishing to join contacts a WIR office and

(Box 3 continued) sets up a meeting at which the firm's credit requirements and the collateral it is able to offer are discussed. As first mortgages in Switzerland do not usually exceed 60% of the purchase price of a property, the collateral most frequently offered is a second mortgage on a house or business premises. In recent years, over 80% of WIR's loans have been secured this way. A loan application is then sent to the WIR credit approval committee; this checks the security and obtains a report on the applicant from a credit-checking agency. If the report and the security are in order, the new participant is given a WIR chequebook, a plastic charge card and a large catalogue listing other participants with whom the loan can be spent.

Although the sums in WIR accounts are denominated in Swiss francs they cannot be turned into normal currency, paid into ordinary banks or given to non-members. Even when someone wishes to leave the organization, they cannot exchange the system's units (Wir) for national currency. As a result, the purchasing power created when the credit committee authorizes a loan remains entirely within the 'ring', generating increased business for all participants. Secured loans of this type are cheap. In 1994, Wir mortgages carried a service charge of 1.75% and relatively long repayment terms could be negotiated; the charge for ordinary current-account loans was 2.5%.

Almost every conceivable product and service is available through WIR, whose members in a recent year included 167 lawyers, 16 undertakers, 1,853 architects and 18 chimney sweeps. Not all suppliers take 100% payment in Wir, but with several sources listed for most products and services, it is generally possible to find at least one who will (especially at slack times of year or during sales).

Overall, the Wir avoids the two main defects of national currencies: it is never in short supply, and because no interest is charged for its use it does not create the growth compulsion. In addition, it does not have to be earned or borrowed from outsiders before it can be used. Its main drawback seems to be that it is often regarded as a way of financing the working capital requirements of businesses, rather than purely of facilitating trade between them. As a result, too many long-term loans are issued and some members earn so many units that they become reluctant to take any more. The availability of mortgages has obviously compounded this problem.

it in the warehouse but knew that it would deteriorate there. Consequently people used the commodity themselves, or spent the receipts, as soon as reasonably possible. As a result, money was not hoarded but circulated well.

Shell money performed well

The earliest account of the use of wampum (the shells of a clam, *Venus Mercenaria*) as money in North America dates from 1535. Both native Americans and the European settlers used the shells, and they were made legal tender for payments of up to a shilling in Massachusetts in 1637. This limit was raised to £2 in 1643, a substantial sum at the time as it was equivalent to three week's wages for a skilled man. Although wampum ceased to be legal tender in the New England states in 1661, the last factory drilling the shells and putting them on strings for use as money closed as late as 1860. In the early days, several coastal tribes such as the Narragansetts specialized in making up the strings and exchanging them for goods with settlers and inland tribes who wished to have the convenience of a means of exchange.

The essential feature of all these commodity currencies is that they were open to anyone with time and access to land or seashore to produce. This didn't mean, however, that they could be produced without out cost and that the money supply was therefore unlimited. If that had been the case, the monetary unit would have had no value. The currencies worked because people would only spend their time making tokens to serve as money if that was the best way of satisfying their needs. In other words, whenever they could get their needs (food, clothing, shelter) more easily by growing them or collecting them themselves (instead of

"Then it's agreed. Until the dollar firms up, we let the clamshell float."
Drawing by Ed Fisher; © 1971 *The New Yorker Magazine, Inc.*

growing tobacco, or collecting wampum shells to trade), they would obviously do so. As a result, money was only produced and spent into circulation when its exchange rate with real goods was favourable, a feature that generally guaranteed that it would maintain its value. There were exceptions to this, of course. The value of gold in terms of the goods it would buy fell in Europe when the Spanish conquistadors brought in plundered supplies from South America. Similarly, the exchange rate of wampum against commodities such as beaver pelts dropped sharply when the European settlers began using steel drills to bore the stringing holes. This was because they could produce them much faster (and therefore with a reduced opportunity cost) than the Indians using stone-tipped tools.

A non-commodity currency

Although the value of their units is not based on any commodity, Local Exchange and Trading Systems (LETS) are a modern equivalent of wampum and the other types of popularly-produced money because they enable people to create spending units for themselves. They are generally set up by a group of people living in the same area who have time on their hands and too little national currency to meet their requirements. The first system was set up in the early 1980s in British Columbia by Michael Linton, as a response to the unemployment caused when a local air base closed down.

Over a thousand communities throughout the world have LETS systems, and many variants on the original model have been developed. The common feature of every LETS, however, is that members trade with each other using a monetary unit of their own devising (often called odd names like Hags, Bats, Bobbins and Reeks) and that records are kept of all transactions. This makes it possible to spot members who are taking more value out of the system than they are putting in.

In a LETS system, members create spending power by going into debt, just as with WIR (see Box 3). When a system starts up, all the participants have a zero balance in their accounts. The first trade between members means that the balance in the account of the member who made the first payment becomes negative, while the account run by the member who supplied goods or services in exchange for that payment becomes positive by the same amount.

The member with the positive balance can then spend the units with other members, while the member with a negative balance will have to supply goods or services to someone else in the system to return their account to zero, or to get into the positive zone.

In most cases, payments between members of a LETS system are made using cheques that are sent to the system's book-keeper who credits and debits accounts. In some systems, however, payment information is simply telephoned to the book-keeper, or his or her answering machine. In a few systems, fixed-value tokens (i.e. scrip) circulate between members to cut out the book-keeping that would be entailed by a lot of small cheque transactions. Just as happens with national currency, members get these tokens from their system's bank and their accounts are debited with the amount involved. If members earn tokens they don't want, they can lodge them to their accounts for credit. The use of scrip is very common among LETS systems in Argentina.

Perhaps the best system for keeping LETS accounts evolved in Germany in 1997. In exchange for their annual membership fee, members receive a record book. When they go to work for another member, or sell them something, the other member writes the details and the amount of the transaction in their book, and signs it while they write in the other member's. This means that the balance of each member's account is always up to date. The record books are exchanged for new ones at the end of each year and they are checked by the managing committee to ensure that no fraud has occurred.

LETS systems' major weakness

Besides eliminating centralized account keeping, the German-style record books have the potential to ameliorate a major weakness in most LETS systems. Linton's original philosophy was that it should be left to each member to decide how much indebtedness they could take on. If other members, knowing the state of the member's account, then sanctioned his or her decision to take on more debt by selling more of their goods and services, that was all right.

This has not worked well, however. Indeed, a major factor in the collapse of Linton's pioneering system after a few year's trading was the high level of indebtedness of Linton's personal account. Nevertheless, many systems have continued to adopt this approach.

True, some do impose credit limits but none seems to have found a satisfactory way of ensuring that members do not stay permanently in deficit. As a result, members whose accounts are in credit frequently find their units are difficult to spend because indebted members see little reason, apart from mild group pressure, to go out of their way to earn them. The members in credit consequently become disenchanted with the system and leave. With the German-type record books, however, it would be a simple matter to prohibit members from selling to people whose account-books showed them to be overdrawn beyond an agreed figure. Requiring overdrawn members to get back into credit within a certain time would still be a problem, however.

Because of their reliance on these lax informal controls, very few LETS systems have been able to recruit and retain more than 200 active members. This has meant that their economic effects have been small, but they nevertheless play a very valuable social network-building role for people on the social and economic fringes of their communities. Bigger, more economically effective systems would require legally enforceable agreements backed by collateral, similar to those adopted by WIR.

By allowing people to trade using monetary units they have generated themselves, LETS systems meet the need that wampum strings, or wheat deposit certificates, met in earlier times. But there are important differences. For example, wampum shells allowed their holders to trade beyond their communities, while LETS systems are used to enable people to trade within them. In addition, LETS systems, like the WIR, have no need to establish the value of their unit by requiring people to do a certain amount of work to produce them. They normally use the value of their national currency unit as their measuring stick, although some systems have experimented with units based on time (for instance, Time Dollars—a community currency system in which people provide each other with care, in which everyone's hourly rate is the same). This saves the effort that has to be wasted on producing, in the case of gold, Yap stones and wampum, commodities that would be unnecessary but for their monetary use. The downside, however, is the fact that indebtedness levels need to be policed, as we have just discussed.

So let's answer our eight questions about popularly produced currencies:

Question 1: Who creates the money?—With the commodity-based currencies, anyone with time and access to resources. With LETS and WIR, it is the members.

Question 2: Why do they create money?—To facilitate their own trading.

Question 3: How do they create money?—With the commodity-based currencies, by producing tokens which embody a fixed amount of labour and resources. With LETS and WIR, by granting members the right to borrow up to a certain amount. No interest is charged on these borrowings. Only a service charge to cover the costs of running the system is paid.

Question 4: When do they create money? With the commodity-based currencies, whenever it is more advantageous to produce more currency than to produce other goods and services. With LETS, whenever a member wishes to trade and other members, or the committee, allows them to create the units to do so. With WIR, whenever the management thinks that the demand for loans can be satisfied without putting too much extra spending power into the system. If the latter happens, then members with positive balances in their accounts will be reluctant to accept more Wir as they cannot find attractive ways of spending them.

Question 5: What gives the money its value? With gold, Yap stones and wampum, purely their acceptability to others. Their exchange value for other commodities or labour is not guaranteed. Wheat, tobacco and other consumable commodity-based currencies are backed by the amount of the commodity the receipt represents. Their exchange value for the purchase of other commodities will fluctuate quite widely from year to year, according to relative growing and harvest conditions. With LETS and WIR, the value of a unit is determined by the readiness of other members of the system to provide their goods and services in exchange for it at its nominal value in the national currency. The range of goods and services available in exchange is also a consideration.

Question 6: Where is the money created?

Within the group of people or the territory using it. It does not have to be earned or borrowed from outside first.

Question 7: How well does the money work?

A: As a means of exchange? Gold does not work well as a means of exchange unless it is turned into coins, something that is discussed in the next chapter. Moreover, the supply of coins has often been inadequate for the amount of trade desired, forcing people to barter, or use a range of gold-substitutes. Yap stones seem to have played the role of large denomination notes, only useful for major purchases, which is why mats, ginger and shells were required as small change. Wampum strings were designed to make counting easy and obviously performed well since they survived in use in competition with other currencies for hundreds of years. The Egyptian grain and the New England tobacco receipts also worked well and sophisticated money transfer systems developed for them. It would, however, be a mistake to establish commodity-based currencies in economies that were not dominated by the production of that commodity, and that were consequently not prepared to allow all price relationships to vary according to its level of production. LETS units perform poorly as a means of exchange because of the lack of pressure on those in debt to earn them. Their use is also restricted to a small group. Wir are better than LETS but still work significantly less well than the Swiss franc, as they are only acceptable among a particular group. As a result, users frequently want to exchange their Wir for Swiss francs and, breaking their system's rules, sell them at a discount to do so.

B: As a unit of account? Only the Wir scores highly here. It functions as well as the Swiss franc since, unless a firm wishes, there is no need for it to distinguish between the two in its books. LETS units are never worth as much as the national currency they shadow, and the gap between the two is variable, depending on a system's membership and its attitude at the time. The gluts and shortages caused by differing harvests, gold rushes and technological change mean that the value of the commodity-based currencies in terms of other goods and services is too erratic to provide a good accounting base.

C: As a store of value? Gold proved an excellent store of value between 1658 and 1798, fluctuating by no more than a third during this time. The discovery of the cyanide method of extracting it from crushed rock in 1887, coupled with major finds between 1847-97 increased production enormously. This damaged it as a store of value. The world's gold stock is estimated to have doubled between 1890-1914 allowing prices in Britain to rise by 25%, and in the US by 40%. If powered equipment had been used it would undoubtedly have lowered the value of Yap stones too, and as we have already seen, steel drill bits devalued wampum. All commodity-based currencies have the defect that their value will fall if the commodity on which they are based becomes cheaper to produce. The Exeter Constant[19] was an experimental currency used in New Hampshire (in the US) for a year in 1972-3, whose value in dollar terms was based on the current market price of specific amounts of thirty commodities. It would have lost almost 20% of its purchasing power in terms of other things between 1990-99 because of the extent to which commodity prices fell. LETS units are a hopeless store of value, since one cannot predict if the system will still be in operation in a few years. Like LETS, the Wir is also money that should be spent quickly, although it holds its value reasonably well from year to year. The drawback with it as a form of saving is that, as no interest is paid on accounts in credit, people with a lot of Wir usually want to convert them to Swiss francs to take advantage of the much wider range of investment opportunities in that currency.

Question 8: Is popularly produced money compatible with sustainability? Yes, in all cases, because the availability of these monies only increases when the systems in which they operate have underused resources, particularly those of human labour. In other words, these monies tend to keep the level of economic activity in step with its technological and resource base. And, because these monies are spent into circulation, the constant payment of interest on almost all the money stock entailed by the present system is avoided. This means that the economic systems they produce would not depend on continual expansion in order to avoid a collapse.

Chapter 3

Government-produced Money

Although it was open to anyone to find gold and silver, it was not possible for everyone to turn it into useful money. The problem with simply using a lump of either metal for a transaction was that it could have been adulterated with other, cheaper, substances. Moreover, lumps weren't exactly the right weight for every purchase. Andrew Carnegie, the steel magnate and philanthropist, wrote a book about money a century ago in which he described receiving his change in China as 'shavings and chips cut off a bar of silver and weighed before my eyes on the scales of the merchant.' "The Chinese have no 'coined' money," he explained, "You can well see how impossible it was for me to prevent the Chinese dealer from giving me less than the amount of silver to which I was entitled." Perhaps that was because he was a tourist. Another Chinese merchant would certainly have ensured that he received the right amount.

The twin problems of purity and weight were partially solved by the invention of coins. These were standard-sized pieces of metal, containing a specific amount of gold or silver, stamped with the profile of the head of the state (or the symbol of the temple) that had issued them as a guarantee. The first records of coins of any sort are in China, almost 3,000 years ago: Chinese rulers from the 12th century BC until 1912 (despite Carnegie's remark) regulated the production of small, round, low value, base metal coins with holes for stringing known as 'cash'. Other types of non-round, base metal Chinese coins, inscribed with an official authorization go back much earlier. As China only began making high value silver coins in 1890 (after Carnegie's visit), very large quantities of cash were required to make substantial purchases. Its cash coins had no 'intrinsic' value, any more than a shell currency had in the past, or a pound coin has today.

Currency as a form of tax

Rulers in almost every country have used the currency they issued as a form of tax (see Box 4 on pages 48-9). In 17th century Russia, for example, Tsar Alexis thought that he could mint 312 roubles out of five roubles' worth of copper, while Peter the Great debased his silver coinage by 42%. Their goal was to maximize seigniorage—the difference between the price they had to pay for the metals their mints used, and the spending power of the coins made from them. However there were other, more effective, ways in which a ruler could raise tax with his right to mint money. Bracteates were thin silver-alloy coins issued between the 12th and 15th centuries by the rulers of the small autonomous states in the Holy Roman Empire. Initially, the coins, which could be broken into four to make change, were valid only for a year and had to be replaced before holders could use them at the big autumn markets in most towns. Moreover, as with the other low value coins issued at the time, whenever a ruler who had issued a batch of bracteates died, all the coins bearing his head became invalid and had to be exchanged (at a 20-25% discount), for new ones bearing his successor's features. For obvious reasons, it wasn't long before rulers began to recall bracteates more frequently, sometimes as often as three times a year. In the 14th century Johann II of Saxony changed his currency no less than 86 times in 36 years.[20]

Since bracteates could lose up to a quarter of their value overnight, people spent them as soon as they could. Once their day-to-day purchases had been made, they used the remainder on improving their houses and property. Even relatively ordinary people were able to afford fine houses during this period, and the tradesmen's guilds were prosperous enough to make gifts of towers, windows and complete chapels to the Church. The construction work meant that there was a high demand for labour, and wages were consequently good: an ordinary day-labourer could expect to earn six or eight groats a week, enough to buy four pairs of shoes or two sheep. Working hours were short, and there were at least ninety religious holidays a year. It was a time of great prosperity, with (in the words of the German commentator Fritz Schwartz, from whom much of this material is taken), "no difference between the farmhouse and castle."[21] Farmers wore coats with golden buttons and had silver buckles on their shoes.

Gold ends a golden age

Ironically, it was gold that brought this golden age to a close. A bracteate was generally "a totally wretched and ugly little disc of metal, very thin, of low fineness", and due to its low silver content and its liability to be devalued, it was useless for international trade. Realizing this, the Genoese and the Florentines issued gold coins in 1252, and Venice followed in 1284. These new coins could act as both a store of value and a means of exchange.[22] They allowed people to build up their assets in ways that did not involve employing others and thus passing their surplus around. Moreover, as the gold coins spread, trading itself became more difficult. "The means of exchange disappeared into socks and mattresses," Schwartz writes, and as money became scarce, interest rates soared, despite the opposition of the Church. Some merchants found it more profitable to sell off their stock and lend out their capital, and a gulf developed between families with an income based on interest and the rest of the population. The demand for labour dropped, wages fell, and unemployment appeared. Moreover, rulers had to find other means of taxation.

Even today, the British government makes a profit out of seigniorage. James Robertson, in a paper based on his written submission to the Bank of England Monetary Policy Committee,[23] states that between January 1998 and January 1999 the value of the notes and coins in circulation in the UK rose by £1,300 million. As the cost to the Bank of England of printing the notes and minting the coins would not have been high, the seigniorage it earned must have been at a similar level. During the same period, the amount of money created by the commercial banks was £52,600 million, forty times the amount of money the state made. Although the sum the banks created was balanced by liabilities, and was not therefore money which belonged to them in the way the profit from issuing coins belonged to the British Government, nevertheless the interest paid provided a substantial income for the institutions involved.

Robertson, like many before him, goes on to argue that rather than this money being created by the banks as a debt (as discussed in Chapter 1), the government should have created it instead. It could have spent this money into circulation in place of some of the money it was collecting in taxes. The banks, he says, rather than creating money, should be limited to credit broking. In other words,

Box 4: Devaluation in Britain through the ages

It was Offa, the king of Mercia, who issued the first silver coins minted in England, in 760 AD. He decreed that 240 pennies should be made from a pound of silver. However, as a result of a series of reductions in its silver content, the value of the penny fell inexorably for the next thousand years. The first devaluation was carried out on the orders of William the Conqueror, who opened a mint at the Tower of London in 1067 and decreed that it would make its pennies out of a Tower pound of silver rather than a troy pound. The Tower pound was 6.5% lighter. He also reduced the purity of the silver itself to 925 parts per thousand. This became known as sterling silver, and coins were made from silver of this standard right up to 1920.

As coins were valued by number rather than weight, it was not just the rulers who had an incentive to reduce the amount of silver they contained—the users did too. They brought their reduction about by clipping or filing the coin's metal away to sell, despite the fact that, if detected, they were liable to the death penalty. It was only in 1663 that the Mint began milling each coin's edges to prevent this being done. Until then, to maintain their appearance, coins were periodically re-minted but without adding any more silver.

The first major reduction in William the Conqueror's standard was in 1343, when the weight of a penny was cut from 22 grains of silver to 20.3. By 1346, it was 20, and in 1351, Edward III reduced it to 18 so that he could produce 293 pennies from every pound of silver. During the next 150 years, the weight of silver in a penny was halved, but the value of the metal in terms of other commodities rose so, as Adam Smith pointed-ed out, the price of wheat scarcely varied from 6s. 8d a quarter throughout the period.[24]

Then came the Great Debasement. In 1542, Henry VIII, sorely in need of funds to fight the French, told the Mint to add six ounces of copper to every 10 ounces of sterling silver it used to make pennies. A few months later, the amount of copper was increased to seven ounces per pound, then to ten, then to twelve and finally under Edward VI, to thirteen. The adulteration enabled the Mint to produce much more money than would otherwise have been possible. Prices doubled, and Ket's Rebellion broke out in 1549 in protest against the domestic inflation. On the foreign exchanges, the pound lost over half its value. A proclamation that a shilling (12d) would henceforward be only worth 9d set off a national

(Box 4 continued) panic. It was left to Elizabeth I to call in all the debased coins, refine out the copper, and re-issue them as 100% sterling silver.

England's first gold coin (a gold penny twice the weight of a silver penny and worth twenty times as much) was issued in 1257 primarily for use in the export trade. Running two coinages whose external value was based on their content of different metals didn't work well. "Even the arrival of one Spanish treasure ship in Cadiz, or the departure of a silver-laden trader for the East, could shift the value-ratio between them by several points", Peter Wilsher wrote in *The Pound in your Pocket*, his excellent history to mark the decimalization of the British currency.[25] This was a drag on commerce, so Sir Isaac Newton was asked for his advice as Master of the Mint. He advised that silver should be dropped and fixed a price for gold, to which the value of all other coins was to be related. His advice was taken, and as Wilsher states: "Trade and society flourished as never before."

they should simply take in deposits from one set of customers and lend them out to others, on exactly the same 100% reserve basis as used by the credit unions and those building societies that have not converted themselves into banks. Robertson advances four arguments for such a change:

1. The money the banks put into circulation is, in fact, created by society. The banks only do the book-keeping that brings it into effect. This money is therefore the property of society and should consequently be treated as a source of public revenue rather than commercial profit.

2. If the state spent the appropriate amount of new money into circulation each year, either taxes could be reduced, or public expenditure increased, or both. The benefit would be substantial as, in the 1998-9 period, in which the UK banks lent roughly an extra £50 billion into existence, government spending in the UK was £300 billion.

3. Allowing the banks the privilege of money creation constitutes a massive subsidy to the financial sector. It therefore distorts the way the economy operates.

4. The necessity to pay interest on almost all the money required to keep the economy running bears more heavily on the poor than the rich. It is effectively a regressive tax.

The first three arguments are sound but I have doubts about the fourth. It is certainly true that the poor pay a greater proportion of their income in interest than the rich. Margrit Kennedy shows that in 1982 only the richest 20% of the German population received more interest than it paid.[26] There is little doubt that the same is true in other countries. In the US, for example, the bottom 10% has negative net worth (that is, they owe more money than they could raise if they sold everything they had). In addition, as they are perceived as high-risk borrowers they will certainly be paying a lot of interest on their debts. The fact that money ceased to be created as debt would not cure this problem, however, as borrowing and the payment of interest would still go on. Robertson, though, thinks that ceasing to create money via debt would ease the situation quite a lot, especially if the seigniorage gained by the state when it spent its money into circulation was used to finance the payment of a citizen's income.[27]

Two further arguments were identified in Chapter 1, which could be added to Robertson's list as numbers 5 and 6. In addition, Brian Leslie, the editor of the British Green Party's Land Tax and Economics Policy Working Group newsletter, *Sustainable Economics*, has suggested the seventh argument, which I believe carries a great deal of weight.[28]

5. If new money were spent into circulation rather being created as debt, the money stock would not contract if, as a result of a change in the economic climate, less borrowing was undertaken and less investment carried out. As a result, the potential level of profit would remain the same. This is a big advantage, as it would make the economy much more stable than it is at present. If firms in a particular industry got into difficulties and went into liquidation, their departure would leave the same money supply, and thus the same potential level of purchasing power, to be shared among the rest of the economy. Demand in other sectors would therefore increase and profits rise, tending to counteract the decline.

6. Spending money into circulation creates a stable economic system that does not have to be kept constantly growing regardless of the environmental and social consequences. Such a system is therefore more sustainable.

7. Because a high volume of bank lending is required to keep the present money system functioning, the banks shape the way the economy develops. This is because they determine who can borrow, and for what purposes, according to criteria that favours those with a strong cash flow and/or substantial collateral. As a result, the present money system favours multinational companies and the rich, and discriminates against smaller firms and poorer individuals. The proposed system of money creation would lessen this bias.

The power of these arguments seems irresistible and I wholeheartedly support Robertson's proposals. The only problem that might arise is that governments could become addicted to economic growth not because it was proving beneficial, but because the increase in the money supply the growth necessitated was an important source of tax revenue. A no-growth economy that was not inflating would not need a larger money supply each year and, consequently, the government's earnings from seigniorage would cease. Robertson is aware of this and knows that governments will be constantly tempted (as were the kings before them) to collect seigniorage by increasing the money supply in circumstances in which no extra liquidity is warranted. The attractions of creating a mini-boom just ahead of a general election would be especially hard to resist. He therefore proposes that decisions on money creation should be taken by an independent body and thus removed from direct political control.

Proposed world currency system

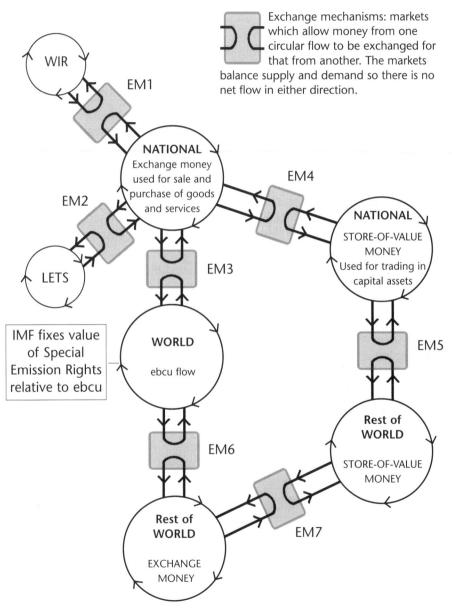

Exchange mechanisms: markets which allow money from one circular flow to be exchanged for that from another. The markets balance supply and demand so there is no net flow in either direction.

WIR

EM1

NATIONAL
Exchange money used for sale and purchase of goods and services

EM4

EM2

NATIONAL
STORE-OF-VALUE MONEY
Used for trading in capital assets

LETS

EM3

IMF fixes value of Special Emission Rights relative to ebcu

WORLD
ebcu flow

EM5

Rest of WORLD
STORE-OF-VALUE MONEY

EM6

Rest of WORLD
EXCHANGE MONEY

EM7

For an explanation of the various Exchange Mechanisms, see Appendix I.

Chapter 4

One Country, Four Currencies

Now we've surveyed the various types of money system, we come to the exciting bit: specifying the integrated multi-currency system of the future. We have seen that three groups (commercial institutions, governments and users) can create money, and that very little can be said in favour of allowing the commercial creation of money to continue. Instead, money should be created by non-profit-seeking organizations representing the people using it. In the case of a democratic country, this would obviously include a national, or regional, government working on behalf of its people.

At least four types of money are needed. One is an international currency, playing the role taken by gold before the collapse of the gold exchange standard. The second is a national or regional (subnational) currency that would relate to the international currency in some way. Thirdly, we would need a plethora of currencies which, like LETS, the Wir and the commodity-based currencies, could be created at will by their users to mobilize resources left untapped by national or regional systems. Many of these user currencies would confine their activities to particular geographic areas, but some would link non-spatially-based communities of interest. And fourth, as our current money's store of value function can so easily conflict with its use as a means of exchange, special currencies are needed for people wishing to see their savings hold their value while still keeping them in a fairly liquid form.

1. An international currency, the ebcu
The dollar, the pound sterling, the franc, the German and Swiss marks and the yen are all 'reserve currencies'. In other words, central banks keep their reserves in these currencies, in case they have to intervene in the markets to support the exchange rates of their own currency. A country operating a reserve currency has an enormous advantage because other countries willingly sell it their goods

and services but don't use a lot of the money they receive to buy its goods and services in exchange. Instead, they leave the money sitting in their central banks. Holders aren't even paid interest by the country that issued the currency.

In addition, reserve currencies are used as world money. For instance commercial banks in Europe accept deposits of dollars and lend them out to other customers who, rather than using them for purchases in the US, frequently pay suppliers in third countries instead. This enables the dollars to circulate without ever returning to a US bank. Such dollars are known as Euro-dollars, but Euro-versions of the pound, the Deutsche mark (D-mark), the Swiss franc and the yen also exist. On a more basic level, people use reserve currencies for day-to-day transactions in countries experiencing high rates of inflation. Others often keep foreign notes as a standby.

At the end of 1998, 57% of the world's foreign exchange reserves were held in dollars, around three times the amount held in ecus, D-marks, French francs and sterling combined. This means that, over the years, the US has received billions of dollars worth of imports and given nothing in return apart from paper notes and electronic credits. Its earnings from seigniorage have been massive; and an important reason for the launch of the Euro was that it stands an excellent chance of displacing the dollar as the world's preferred reserve currency and thus earning for the EU a much bigger share of the seigniorage gains.

Allowing the world's rich countries to profit from poorer ones in this way is obviously wrong. Moreover it flies in the face of the principle that we've just established, namely that money should be created and its supply controlled by its users and not, as in this case, nations making huge profits for themselves.

Which scarce resource?

Chapter One argued that every economic system should establish the scarce resource whose use it seeks to minimize, and then adjust its systems and technologies to bring the least-use solution about. Since people always try to minimize their expenditure, an international currency should be based on the global resource whose use it is highly desirable to minimize. If that link was made, anyone minimizing their use of money would automatically minimize their use of the scarce resource.

If we accept that view (and not everyone does), what resources do we need to use less of? Certainly not labour or capital goods. There is worldwide unemployment and, in comparison with a century ago, our capital stock is huge and underused. But the natural environment is grossly overused, particularly as a dump for our pollutants. In particular, the Intergovernmental Panel on Climate Change (IPCC) believes that 60-80% cuts in emissions of greenhouse gases—pollutants which are produced largely a result of fossil fuel use—are urgently needed to lessen the risk of a runaway global warming. This is one of humankind's most serious problems, and I therefore believe that the base of the world currency should be selected accordingly.

But how can a link between a currency and lower fossil fuel use be made? If the currency we have in mind were linked to a unit of energy, that would effectively encourage more energy production throughout the world. We want to achieve quite the reverse and to link our monetary unit to something that discourages fossil fuel use even when there is pressure for an expansion of the amount of money in circulation.

How can this be done? Contraction and Convergence (C&C) is a plan for reducing greenhouse gas emissions developed by the Global Commons Institute in London; by early 1999 it had gained the support of the majority of the world's nations. Under the C&C approach, the international community agrees how much the CO_2 level in the atmosphere can be allowed to rise. There is considerable uncertainty over this. The EU considers a doubling from pre-industrial levels to around 550 parts per million (ppm) might be safe, while Bert Bolin, the former chairman of the IPCC, has suggested that 450 ppm should be considered the absolute upper limit. Even the present level of roughly 360ppm may prove too high, though, because of the time lag between a rise in concentration and the climate changes it brings about.

Whatever CO_2 concentration target is ultimately chosen automatically sets the number of years within which the world must reduce its present emissions by whatever amount is necessary to bring them into line with the Earth's capacity to absorb the gas. So, if a decision to cut emissions by a fixed proportion each year is made, a maximum level of CO_2 emissions for the world for each year for at least the next fifty years can be calculated.

Once the annual global limits have been set, the right to burn whatever amount of fuel has been fixed for each year would be shared out among the nations of the world on the basis of their population in a certain base year. In the early stages of the contraction process, some nations would find themselves consuming less than their allocation, and others more, so it is proposed that under-consumers should have the right to sell their surplus to more energy-intensive lands. This is a key feature of the scheme as it would generate an income for some of the poorest countries in the world and give them an incentive to continue following a low-energy development path. Eventually, it is likely that most countries will converge on similar levels of fossil energy use per head.

But what currency are the over-consuming nations going to use to buy extra CO_2 emission permits? If they used their reserve currencies, they would effectively get the right to use a lot of their extra energy for free. This is because much of the money they paid would be used as an exchange currency around the world, rather than being used to purchase goods from the country that issued it. To avoid this, GCI has devised a plan under which an international organization such as the International Monetary Fund (IMF) would assign Special Emission Rights (SERs)—the right to emit a specified amount of greenhouse gases and hence to burn fossil fuel—to national governments every month according to the C&C formula.

Energy coupons

SERs would essentially be ration coupons, to be handed over to fossil-fuel production companies in addition to cash by big users such as electricity companies, and by fuel distributors such as oil and coal merchants. An international inspectorate would monitor producers to ensure that their sales did not exceed the number of SERs they received. This would be surprisingly easy, as nearly 80% of the fossil carbon that ends up as man-made CO_2 in the earth's atmosphere comes from only 122 producers of carbon-based fuels.[29] The used SER coupons would then be destroyed.

A considerable amount of work has already been done towards the development of an international trading system in CO_2 emission rights, both at a theoretical level and in practice in the US. There, trading in permits entitling the bearer to emit sulphur dioxide into the atmosphere has led to a rapid reduction in discharges at the lowest possible cost. The Futures Exchange in Sydney, Australia, is planning to start trading in mid-2000 in the CO_2 that projects have saved.

David Fleming, an independent economist living in London, has been working out how the SERs would operate at a national level. He envisages that perhaps 45% of each country's allocation would be shared out equally among its population in the form of 'domestic tradable quotas' (DTQs). These would have to be surrendered in addition to cash whenever people purchased electricity or fuel. In advanced countries, people could have their DTQs paid into accounts similar to those for their credit and debit cards. The accounts would be topped-up each month. All forms of fuel and energy, including renewables, would be rated for their emissions of global warming gases. When people bought them they would use paper tokens, or their special debit card, to pay over DTQ units in line with those ratings. People who were able to stay within their allocation would be able to sell their surplus units, while those who needed to buy more would be able to do so through a bank or post office, exactly as with foreign currencies.

The remaining 55% of the national allowance would be auctioned to all other users, such as industry, institutions and the government itself, and the revenue used to finance an emergency renewable energy development and conservation programme.

Besides the SERs, the IMF would issue governments with energy-backed currency units (ebcus) on the same per capita basis, and hold itself ready to supply additional SERs to whoever presented it with a specific amount of ebcus. This would fix the value of the ebcu in relation to a certain amount of greenhouse emissions, and subsequently to the use of fossil energy.

The ebcu issue would be a once off, to get the system started. If a government actually used ebcus to buy additional SERs from the IMF in order to be able to buy more fossil energy, the number of ebcus in circulation internationally would not be increased to make up for the loss. Instead, the ebcus paid over would simply be cancelled and the world would have to manage with less ebcus in circulation. In other words, the IMF's obligation to supply additional SERs would be strictly limited by the amount of ebcus it put into circulation. There would be no open-ended commitment.

Governments would not have to distribute all their allocation of SERs to their citizens, or auction them to major energy users. They would also have the option of selling them to other governments for ebcus. The price set by these sales would establish the exchange rate of their national exchange currencies (see Section 2 below) in terms of ebcus, and thus in terms of other national exchange currencies. This is because if the price that large-scale energy users were prepared to pay at auction for a 1000-tonne SER was, say, £10,000 and the government could sell that SER on the world market for 500 ebcu, each ebcu would be worth £20. This would set the prices for imports and exports, as these would also be paid for in ebcus.

Controlling energy rather than credit

Under this system, countries would control their economies by adjusting the energy supply rather than the credit supply as they do today. Suppose a government sold more of this month's SER allocation on the world market than it did of last month's. This would increase the supply of ebcus being exchanged for national exchange currency, thus tending to make imports cheaper and exports more expensive. Within the country itself, however, output would drop as, with less energy available, the ability of people to produce would fall. Since there would be a fixed amount of the exchange currency in circulation, the price of the reduced output would be pushed up, and people would switch to buying more of the now-cheaper imports. The higher domestic prices would allow the big energy purchasers to bid more at the next SER auction, thus offering the government a better price than it could obtain from international buyers and encouraging it not to sell as much abroad the following month. The increased demand for imports and the lower level of exports because of the higher domestic prices would also tend to devalue the national exchange currency in terms of the ebcu. In other words, both feedbacks would be negative, tending to restore the system to balance. Similarly, if the government decided to buy extra SERs, the purchases would mean that there would be fewer ebcus available for normal trade, with the result that the price of the remainder would rise in terms of the national exchange currency. This would encourage exports and deter imports until the balance was restored.

The result would be much the same if a country put so much of its exchange currency into circulation that the economy expanded faster than the rate at which it became more energy-efficient, causing the demand for fossil energy to rise. This increased demand would allow energy companies to increase their prices, thus causing inflation that, by making exporting more difficult and encouraging imports, would cut the level of economic activity in the country and thus its level of energy use. In other words, national economies could only expand at the rate they became more fossil-energy efficient, which is just what we want. And, for the first time since the gold exchange standard was abandoned, both the international and the national currency would represent something real, although the latter's value in terms of the former would not, as we have seen, be fixed. The system would be nicely self-balancing but would cause inflation whenever it operated.

There is a possibility that, if world energy efficiency could not be

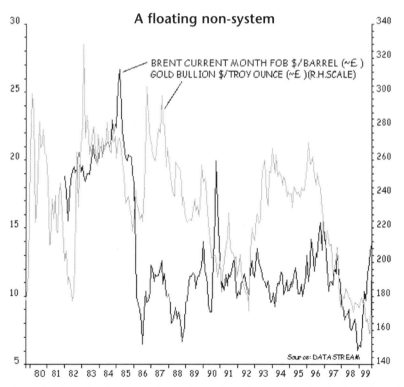

A floating non-system

BRENT CURRENT MONTH FOB $/BARREL (~£)
GOLD BULLION $/TROY OUNCE (~£)(R.H.SCALE)

Source: DATA STREAM

Since the fixed link between the dollar and gold was cut in 1971, the value of the dollar has fluctuated widely in terms of the amount of gold and oil it can buy.

Box 5: The end of the two Gold Standards

The gold standard worked reasonably well up to 1914, but was cast aside by all the major combatants except the US during the First World War. It proved impossible to restore during the 1920s and 30s, although great efforts were made to do so. Churchill, for example, insisted in 1925 that Britain should restore convertibility between the pound sterling and gold at the pre-war level of 123.3 grains of gold at eleven-twelfths fine to £1. This required the British price level to be cut by between 10-15% if export competitiveness was to be maintained. The attempt to deflate by this amount caused the General Strike in 1926 and massive unemployment. Keynes wrote later of "the disastrous inefficiency which the international gold standard has worked since its restoration five years ago . . . and the economic losses, second only to those of a great war, which it has brought upon the world." Even the US was forced off the gold standard in 1933.

After the Second World War, the non-communist industrialized nations adopted the gold exchange standard rather than the gold standard. Under this, they fixed their exchange rates in relation to the US dollar, which itself was fixed in terms of gold. However, the US, as the world's banker, did what many goldsmiths had done previously and failed to observe a sufficiently cautious ratio between the number of dollars it allowed its commercial banks to put into circulation, and its reserves of gold. Confidence in the ability of the US to maintain the fixed exchange rate between the dollar and gold was finally destroyed by the surge of money that went into circulation in the US to cover the costs of fighting the Vietnam war. All around the world, holders of dollars rushed to convert them to gold.

On August 15th, 1971, President Nixon cracked. He took the US off the gold exchange standard, thus removing the last fixed link between the world's money and anything real. By doing so he created "a floating non-system" as the then German Chancellor called it.

Ever since then, the value of currencies has fluctuated in response to the whims of the market to an unprecedented extent. Central banks are forced to adjust interest rates and the amount of money in circulation in their domestic economies on the basis of how those economies are perceived internationally, rather than the volume of trade going on. This obviously severely damages their currencies' ability to serve as a satisfactory medium of exchange.

increased as fast as the monthly supply of SERs was reduced, the price of an SER would rise in terms of ebcus until it reached the price at which the IMF was prepared to sell additional SERs. If such sales were made and the ebcus involved withdrawn from global circulation, the world's money stock would be reduced. This would cut the amount of trading it was possible to carry on and, as a result, the level of fossil energy consumption would fall as well.

Essentially, the proposed system is a version of the gold exchange standard (see Box 5 opposite) in which the right to burn fossil energy has replaced the yellow metal, and where ebcus play the role of the US dollar. This might lead traditionalists to suggest that the world should go back to the real gold standard rather than an ersatz one but, apart from the aura surrounding the metal, it is hard to see why it should. The following arguments all stand against it:

1. Expending energy and effort on mining the metal would be as wasteful as making Yap stones.

2. The supply, and therefore the value of gold in terms of all other commodities, is liable to fluctuate unpredictably because new techniques and new mines can increase its availability at any time. The recent development of heap leaching made gold less costly to extract.

3. Gold production is mainly concentrated in seven countries: South Africa, Russia, Indonesia, China, Uzbekistan, Brazil and Peru. Thus, remonetarizing gold would chiefly benefit only these countries rather than, as in the case of the ebcu, the whole of the non-industrial world.

4. A return to gold would do nothing to make the distribution of global income any less unfair. It would also do nothing to protect the global environment. Indeed, it would increase pressures on the natural world as gold mining causes serious environmental damage.

1. National and regional exchange currencies

The function of these currencies would be solely as a means of exchange. They would not attempt to be a unit of account, nor a store of value. The unit of account function would be filled by the ebcu, and businesses would convert the balances from their books (kept in their national exchange currencies) into ebcus at the end of each accounting period. Turnover and profits or losses would therefore be comparable across national borders.

As discussed in the last chapter, exchange currencies would be created by each country's central bank and spent into circulation by the regional or national governments' spending departments such as education, health and social welfare. If this spending was excessive, or some other factor caused the national economy to inflate, there would be no means of withdrawing the excess currency from circulation to damp things down apart from increasing tax rates and/or cutting government spending so as to run a budget surplus. This is because governments would no longer permit open market operations (the buying and selling of bonds currently carried out by central banks) to control the amount of money in circulation.

There are several reasons for wanting such a ban. One is that an exchange currency is not the right vehicle for bonds, or other long-term savings, which would be kept in a store-of-value currency (see Section 4 below) instead. The only loans in the exchange currency that would be permitted would be to cope with short-term imbalances between receipts and expenditure. These might be limited to less than a year. Banning open market operations would also allow the interest rates on savings in the store-of-value currency to be determined solely by the supply of funds, and the risk and potential return of the projects proposed at the time. In other words, the allocative function of interest would work properly as the capital market would not be constantly blown hither and thither by control-of-money-supply considerations.

The benefits of inflation

Under the new system of issuing exchange money, many central banks would be happy to allow low levels of inflation to occur. This is because, as currency managers, they would they see their primary job as ensuring that enough national exchange currency was always available to create easy trading conditions. Because another currency was providing the store of value, they would not be overly concerned about preserving the purchasing power of their currency, provided that it was not inflating so rapidly that it was becoming less acceptable in the market place. Moreover, they would welcome the seigniorage that inflation enabled them to earn. And, if an inflation did occur, most governments, rather than raising taxes to stop it, would probably allow prices to rise until the cash value of the trading going on was right for the total amount of exchange money in circulation.

We have already seen that an inflation would occur whenever the fossil energy supply was brought into balance with the exchange currency supply, and hence with the level of trading. Such an inflation, provided it was not excessive, has advantages besides providing the state with revenue from seigniorage. One is that it ensures that there is a cost to holding money, so that people spend it sooner rather than later, just as they did when bracteates were liable to lose their value overnight. Many readers might be unhappy about this. They could feel that designing a monetary system that deliberately sets out to encourage people to spend is wrong. Under the present system, they know that their spending has an impact on the environment and they feel under a moral obligation to make their personal impact on the planet as light as possible.

Under the new system, however, the most damaging human environmental impact will be reduced automatically year by year, no matter how much spending goes on. Indeed, it will only be by spending on such things as human labour that we will be able to maximize the benefits we obtain from annually reducing the amount of fossil energy burnt. The German currency reformer, Silvio Gesell, saw the damage that the failure to spend money promptly did in the 1920s and 30s and argued that demurrage should be charged to users who delay money. He drew a parallel with the ship owners and railway companies who charge a demurrage fee if a ship or a wagon is delayed by the user's failure to load or unload in the agreed time. Under the current proposals, inflation is used as a handy way to collect such a fee, although there is a side-effect from doing so. A proper demurrage scheme would not affect the price level, while an inflation obviously does.

Another benefit from a mild inflation is that it allows prices to change in relation to each other almost painlessly. For example, it allows firms to make creeping adjustments to wage differentials. This means that workers with skills in short supply can have their real wages raised gradually while those in a declining area of business, people who would never agree to take less money in cash terms, can be given increases of less than the inflation rate. This process signals to the workers in the declining sector that they should seek better-paid jobs and enables the sector to shrink gracefully as its workforce gradually moves to expanding areas of the economy. The lower real wages also allow the declining sector to survive longer. In short, inflation provides a near-painless adjustment mechanism that is going to be almost essential if the massive changes required to enable economies to become sustainable are to be carried out rapidly without causing bankruptcies and labour unrest.

Smaller might be better

Except in the tiniest countries, regional (sub-national) exchange currencies might be better than national ones in meeting users' needs. A drawback that can arise with a national exchange currency, and which is almost inevitable with an international currency such as the Euro, is that if a major crisis, such as the collapse of an important industry, takes place in one region of a country and leaves other regions where the industry was absent unaffected, it is very difficult to attract or grow replacement industries to the affected region. That is, unless its price levels drop, in particular its labour costs. The price levels that need to fall were, of course, set before the industry collapsed but are now too high to make the depressed area the most profitable location for a new, or expanding, business. Moreover, the newly-unemployed in that region will fight against accepting lower wages to 'price themselves back into work' because many will have mortgages or other financial commitments based on their present wages. Consequently, it could be years before the region is able to restore its competitiveness in relation to the rest of the country (or, with the Euro, the rest of Europe) and for its unemployment to begin to fall. Great social distress could arise.

Sub-national exchange currencies would overcome this problem because the fact that the region was exporting less, and importing more, after the industry collapsed would mean that its exchange rate would fall in relation to the ebcu, and thus in relation to the currencies used in the rest of the country. This would restore its competitiveness in a matter of months. If regional currencies had been in operation in Britain in the 1980s, when London boomed while the North of England's economy suffered after the closure of its coal mines and most of its heavy industries, then the North-South gap which developed might have been prevented. The North of England pound could have been allowed to fall in value compared with the London one, saving many of the businesses that were forced to close.

One final point. The market should solely determine the value of national and regional exchange currencies in relation to the ebcu. Central banks should not maintain ebcu and foreign currency reserves for supporting their currencies. Speculators ought to be able to moderate the rate of change of the currencies and prevent them overshooting their new values at least as well as any central bank. In addition, leaving the determination of relative exchange rates strictly to the market would make the establishment of regional currencies a much simpler process as there would be very little financial infrastructure to put in place.

2. User-controlled exchange currencies

Currencies created by users themselves only develop in circumstances in which the national currency is proving inadequate. We have already discussed how the WIR was set up in the currency crisis of the 1930s and how LETS systems are founded by people who have both wants that they would like to fill, and time or other resources for which they cannot find a market in the mainstream economy. In the same way, businesses list their goods and services with barter organizations if they cannot sell them for regular cash. Usually these supplementary currencies are counter-cyclical: they boom when the national economy is depressed, and shrink when it is buoyant.

At this point in the first draft of this paper I wrote: "Countries setting up regional exchange currencies on the lines discussed in the preceding section will not provide a fertile climate for supplementary currencies with a predominantly economic purpose. The regular currency will work too well. On the other hand, supplementary currencies which are primarily social such as Time Dollars will have an important role to play in areas with mobile populations." On reflection, I'm not sure that this is true. The level of activity in the national economy will depend on the amount of fossil fuel available and the efficiency with which it is used. By contrast, the level of activity in the local economy will depend more on human and renewable energies, and on the availability of local resources. If this is correct, there will be a need for local exchange currencies too, and it will be interesting to see how the balance between local and national ones works out.

Box 6: A low-cost way to start a regional currency

The Roma currency system was invented by Gerry McGarry, an Irish engineer, cinema owner and social activist, to encourage the businesses in his area to do more trade among themselves and to raise money for local charities. The first notes went into circulation in a small Irish town, Ballyhaunis, in 1999 and were withdrawn as planned two months later. The experiment raised £1,500 for good causes.

Although Romas can serve as a short-term currency to raise money for a community cause, their potential is far greater as a low-cost, low-risk way of developing a system equivalent to the WIR. They work as follows. Members of voluntary organizations approach businesses in their area asking for gifts of Romas to support their activities. If the trader agrees, the local manager of the Roma system overprints the required number of notes with the name, address and logo of the donor and that of the good cause to which they are being given. The business sponsoring the notes promises to supply goods or services to the value of £1 for every note presented at its premises. It also agrees to honour notes issued by other sponsors.

The notes are also overprinted with a date a few months from the time of issue after which holders can present them to the organizers for conversion into cash at a rate of one Roma to an Irish pound. The cash to cover the cost of conversion comes from the sponsors. If a business has backed, say, £500-worth of Romas that matured last month, it can cover the cost of its sponsorship by paying the organizers £500 in cash, or handing over 500 mature Romas, no matter who issued them. If the business has gained more than 500 mature Romas, it will be paid £1 for every one above the 500 mark.

The reason for converting mature notes into cash and withdrawing them from circulation after a few months is to create space for later issues of notes in favour of other voluntary organizations. Otherwise, the benefits to the good causes would only occur in the early stages of the currency's development while the amount of Romas in circulation was continuing to expand. Notes that aren't presented for conversion within a month of maturity lose their value altogether. This is to allow the accounts for a particular note issue to be closed.

Firms get major advantages from giving their donations in Romas rather than conventional money. For example, when a firm gives cash, the amount involved comes straight out of its profits for the year because it is

(Box 6 continued) paid from the proceeds of sales that have already been made. A gift of Romas, on the other hand, comes out of the profits to be made on future business which the new money will help to generate. Moreover, the fact that a firm's name appears on the note in association with a local good cause is not only good advertising but builds a lot of goodwill. And, finally, the system is very tax-efficient because the notes are treated as discount vouchers when they are used to make a purchase from the firm that issued them. Consequently the amount of the gift is free of VAT. McGarry thinks that if firms find that supporting local organizations with Romas is beneficial then they will be much more generous to them.

The voluntary organizations spend their notes in the local area just as if they were national currency. In Ballyhaunis, 92 out of the 95 local traders were happy to accept them. The public, too, was happy to earn them, or to take them as change, as they knew that by doing so they were helping the good causes named on them and that they could always spend the notes at the next shop.

The plan is to set up a user-owned co-operative to run the system which will steadily increase the amount of Romas in circulation until saturation is reached and people begin to be reluctant to handle more. Other towns in the area will be brought into the system and the stage should quickly be reached at which notes are being issued and withdrawn every month. After two or three years, when confidence in the Roma as an exchange currency is sufficiently high, the co-op will open cheque accounts for businesses to allow them to pay each other in Roma instead of Irish pounds. These accounts will be operated on the same no-interest, service-charge-only basis as the WIR, and participating firms will be required to give security for overdrafts above a certain amount. There will also be stringent safeguards to ensure that firms spend as many Roma-days in credit as in debit.

When this stage is reached, the ability to accept payments in Roma should give local businesses a competitive advantage within their own area over firms from outside who will have to insist on 100% payment in Irish pounds or, by then, Euros. It will also mean that the people of the area will no longer have to earn money outside the district before they can do business among themselves. The most remarkable thing about the Roma system, however, is that it is simple to set up and cheap to operate and could be developed over a period of years into a fully-fledged regional currency.

3. Store of value currencies

The establishment of a separate store-of-value currency in a nation or region is desirable because it enables the medium-of-exchange currency to work better. One problem with trying to get a single currency to fill both functions is, as we've seen, that if people withdraw money from the circular flow because they want to save/hoard/invest it, they can leave an inadequate amount for trading purposes. This could cause firms to cut their prices to encourage sales, and once people recognize that prices are falling steadily, they will put off buying for as long as they can, thus taking even more money out of the system, reducing purchasing power and making the downturn worse.

Inflation presents another problem to a dual-purpose currency. We just discussed how a moderate level of inflation is desirable because it can help declining sectors of an economy to adjust to changing circumstances. However, any inflation at all means that a currency's store of value is being eaten away. Consequently, it is impossible to strike a perfect balance between the two functions.

Nothing is perfect

There is no such thing as a perfect store of value in this world and there cannot therefore be a perfect store-of-value currency. The exchange value of something is not absolute: it depends on its scarcity and on factors and fashions that vary over time. Putting one's money into real assets, such as property or the stock market, does seem to protect its value in the very long term. Historically, however, there have been periods of two or three decades in which the purchasing power of the assets would have been significantly above or below the initial level. As the graph on page 29 shows, anyone who bought the shares that made up the original Financial Times Index when it was launched, and continually adjusted their portfolio to match it exactly, would have seen the purchasing power of their holding show a loss from 1937-1960 and a gain from 1960-1973. For brief periods the losses were massive: in 1939 the holding would have lost 60% of its value, and in 1975 over 70%. The peak gains were of a similar size, however, and on top of them, dividends would have been paid every year. By contrast, anyone keeping their money in a normal, non-interest-paying account at the bank or under their bed, would have seen its purchasing power fall drastically. Between 1971 to 1991, for example, the Deutsche mark lost more than 52 % of its 1971 value, the US dollar more than 70% and the British pound more than 84%.[30]

There is a precedent for having a currency for spending and a currency for saving, and it seems to have worked well. Between the 1950s and the late 1970s, people who wished to move capital out of the Sterling Area—a group of countries that used sterling for trading among themselves and who often kept their gold and foreign exchange reserves in London—had to buy whatever foreign currency they needed on a special market at a special exchange rate. The rate was quite different from that which applied if they wanted foreign currency for consumption purposes, such as for holidays or for importing goods. The foreign currency they received for a capital transaction, such as the purchase of a holiday home or a business abroad, would have been provided by someone wishing to move their capital in the opposite direction. The exchange rate was determined by supply and demand. Effectively, then, there were two separate types of sterling: capital sterling and consumption sterling. In 1974, when my wife and I sold a house we had built ourselves in Jamaica and brought the Jamaican dollars into the Sterling Area, we received twice as many pounds as would have been the case had we been exchanging the proceeds of an export deal.

The advantage of dividing the foreign exchange market in this way was that capital inflows and outflows always balanced. As a result, capital flows did not distort the exchange rate that applied to imports and exports. However, in the present system the capital and import/export flows are combined. The result is that a big capital inflow discourages exporting by making it less profitable and encourages imports by making them cheaper. New Zealand has suffered badly from this effect. Since the mid-1980s it has sold off its banks, its railways, much of its industry and a lot of its forests to foreign investors, only to see the money they paid strengthening the exchange rate of the New Zealand dollar. This damaged the export earnings of its farmers and encouraged a flood of imports of goods, even soups and other food products previously made at home, sharply increasing the level of unemployment. Quite literally, the country sold its inheritance for, among other things, a mess of pottage.

Storing savings

In the system envisaged in this Briefing, people would want to get any surplus spending power they had out of the exchange currency as quickly as possible because of the rate at which inflation was stripping it of its value. They would therefore convert it into the store-of-value currency at the ruling rate, and either invest the proceeds themselves or hand them over to banks and pension companies to invest for them. Then, when they wanted to spend their savings, they would convert their store-of-value money back into exchange money at whatever the market rate was at the time.

Bank loans, other than less-than-one-year overdraft facilities, would be made in the store-of-value currency which the firm or person taking them out would convert into exchange currency. Interest on these loans, however, would be paid in the exchange currency so that if lenders made a profit after having covered the exchange money costs of their activities, they would have to convert the surplus to store-of-value funds. Similarly, companies would pay dividends on their shares in exchange currency. These arrangements would make it possible to pay interest without either having to increase the amount of exchange money in circulation or reducing the amount in the circular flow. Loan repayments would, of course, have to be made in store-of-value money that the borrower had to buy at the going rate. A futures market would probably appear as soon as the system was adopted, so that borrowers would know exactly what the exchange currency cost of their repayments would be.

People or companies wishing to move their capital out of the region or country would use their store-of-value money to buy foreign store-of-value currency provided by people moving their capital in the other direction, exactly as in the old Sterling Area system. This would prevent a sudden 'capital flight' and make the store-of-value currency very stable without preventing people moving their capital whenever they wished. Another feature contributing to the stability of the store-of-value currency would be that if more people wanted to save rather than to borrow, the exchange rate between the exchange currency and the store of value currency would shift. This would decrease the store-of-value loan required to do a particular job, and thus the amount of exchange currency required to pay the interest on it. This would encourage more people to borrow and fewer to save, bringing supply and demand back into balance.

As I show in my book *Short Circuit*, even flows of capital from one part of a country to another can have damaging consequences.[31] This is because they create employment in the places in which they are invested and thus encourage workers to move to those districts from elsewhere. The arrival of extra people creates further investment opportunities in the areas in which the money was invested. On the other hand, it becomes more difficult to find good investment opportunities in the areas the migrants have left due to the falling population, and these districts start to decline. In other words, a positive feedback builds up, with some places becoming richer while others become poorer. Exactly the same effect can develop between countries if people are able to emigrate. As store-of-value currencies would prevent net capital flows from country to country, they would therefore tend to inhibit the global economic polarization that has recently been taking place.

5. Special purpose currencies

In addition to the four types of money we have mentioned, there would be a need for short-life currencies to fund particular projects. These currencies could perhaps be along the lines of the first stage of the Romas (see Box 6) or the Deli Dollars issued by a delicatessen in Great Barrington, Massachusetts, ten years earlier. The deli faced closure because no bank would advance $4,500 to enable it to move premises. Its dollars were vouchers entitling the bearer to ten dollars worth of food and drink after the delicatessen had relocated. They were sold to customers and the general public at $9 each and became valid for redemption on a staggered basis months later. Enough money was raised to enable the deli to relocate and the notes, although not intended as a currency, circulated as one to a limited extent. It is possible to imagine similar notes being issued to help finance, for example, a wind-energy project. Each note could represent 100Kwh of electricity and be used to pay for it months, or years, later.

The details of possible special currencies are not important at the moment, however. This is because, although they will come in a limited number of basic types, they will exhibit an enormous amount of variation as people adapt them to perform specific functions in many different circumstances. There is little point in speculating on the variations here.

Balancing the global and the local

There would be huge repercussions from introducing the four or five different types of currencies we have discussed. In effect, they would put a semi-permeable membrane around each national or regional exchange currency area. Money, goods and services would be able to pass through these economic membranes, but whatever flows arose would automatically be balanced by an equal flow in the other direction. No longer would the poorer parts of the world be stripped of resources without receiving something of equivalent value.

Similarly, the power that international investors currently have over national governments would be greatly reduced. It would no longer matter whether a big investor moved his money into a country or decided to take it out. The market would ensure that whatever was decided, the external exchange rate of the country's store-of-value currency against other store-of-value currencies would adjust by enough to encourage people to move an equivalent amount of their funds in the opposite direction. As the exchange rate of a country's exchange currency with other exchange currencies would be unaffected by changes in the value of its store-of-value currency, a national or regional government would be able to pursue whatever investor-unfriendly policies it wished, knowing that normal import-export trading would continue.

Globalization would not be dead once international money flows had lost their power to bend national economies to their will, but its source of energy would be gone. As a result, local economies would be able to re-emerge and, protected by their membranes, move towards stability and sustainability as rapidly as they wished. No longer would they fear that moving towards sustainability would lead to their economies being undermined by competition from parts of the world with lower costs from unsustainable production. Instead, in a complete reversal of the present situation, they could look to the financial markets for protection. In the light of this, changing the way money is created is the most important step this generation can take towards securing its own and posterity's future. In Lewis Mumford's phrase, "it is the way to turn a power economy into a life economy."

Chapter 5
Moving On

Many of the ideas in this Briefing are not new. As I pointed out in a reference in Chapter One, in the 1930s Henry Simons and Irving Fisher both urged that US banks should lose the right to create money and that a government-controlled Currency Commission be set up to do so instead. Similarly in 1994 two economists, F.X. Browne and J.P.C. Fell, who then worked for the Central Bank of Ireland but are now employed by the European Central Bank, predicted that at some time in the future the standard of value in which prices would be set, and contracts denominated, would be divorced from the means of payment.[32] They also thought that values would be measured in terms of a unit of account defined in terms of a basket of goods. This is not the same as basing a currency on the right to emit greenhouse gases, of course, but it does involve tying the unit-of-account currency to something real. Their proposal also looks forward to a time in which countries would use two or three currencies for different purposes.

Browne and Fell also suggested that central banks were losing their power to control the money supply. Professor Kevin Dowd of the University of Sheffield agrees.[33] He points out that banks are already providing a smaller proportion of all loans as a result of 'securitization'—the sale of a bank's loans to non-bank investors who are not subject to reserve requirements. This, and the development of electronic cash, means that more and more money can be placed in circulation on a smaller and smaller reserve base. Dowd writes, "As base money becomes less significant, it will gradually lose its effectiveness as a channel through which the central bank can influence the broader money supply".

In other words, our current monetary system is coming to the end of its useful life. Its radical reform has become necessary as well as desirable. Only a widespread debate on the issues, by a well-informed public, will ensure that when changes are made they are along the right lines. ❦

How the Exchange Mechanisms Operate

See the diagram on page 52. All seven exchange mechanisms balance supply and demand by altering the relative price of the pair of currencies being exchanged between them. There is therefore no net movement of currency from one circular flow to another.

EM1 Allows people with earnings in a Wirtschaftsring-type system to exchange them for the national exchange currency, and vice versa.

EM2 Allows members of a LETS to exchange their units for the national exchange currency, and vice versa.

EM3 Ensures that flows of money from imports and exports balance each other. Ebcus from exports and the sale of SERs are exchanged for units of the national exchange currency which people provide in payment for imports and the purchase of SERs.

EM4 Allows people with exchange money they wish to save to swap it for store-of-value money provided by people who need to spend their savings or who have taken out a loan repayable in over twelve months.

EM5 Balances capital flows (which are in the store-of-value currency) into and out of the country.

EM6 Is a composite of all the EM3-type exchanges operated by the rest of the world.

EM7 Balances the flow of money into savings with the flow of money out of savings for the rest of the world.

IMF This is the only fixed point in the systems. If ever the price of an SER in terms of ebcu rises beyond a certain point as a result of exchanges between countries, the IMF will supply SERs and reduce the world's ebcu stock.

Appendix II

References

Foreword

1. J.K. Galbraith, *Money: Whence it came, Where it went,* Houghton Mifflin Co., Boston, 1975, p.5.

Main text

1. M. Neary of the University of Warwick and G. Taylor of the University of the West of England, in their book *Money and the Human Condition,* Macmillan, Basingstoke, 1998.
2. D. Hume, *Of Interest,* 1752.
3. P. A. Samuelson, *Economics, an Introductory Analysis,* McGraw-Hill, New York, 1967.
4. Keynes wrote three books about money: *A Treatise on Money* (1930), *Tract on Monetary Reform* (1923) and *Indian Currency and Finance* (1913), which is noted for its discussion of the gold exchange standard. In his most important book, *The General Theory of Employment, Interest and Money* (Macmillan, London, February 1936, pp.353-8), he discusses Silvio Gesell's ideas for monetary reform. This includes the use of stamped scrip, which was designed to make it costly to hoard money in a period in which prices were falling. Fisher, who was Professor of Economics at Yale University, wrote two books on stamped scrip, *Stamp Scrip* (Adelphi, New York, 1933) and *Mastering the Crisis* (George Allen and Unwin, London, 1934). He also wrote *100% Money* (Adelphi, New York, 1934) which proposed that banks be required to permanently keep on hand reserves of notes and coin equal to the amount that their customers had in their accounts. Simons, who was Professor of Economics at Chicago and taught Milton Friedman, also called for an end to fractional reserve banking. In a 1934 essay included in *Economic Policy for a Free Society* (University of Chicago Press, 1948) he demanded 100% backing of bank deposits and the creation of all currency by the state.

   The only notable economist to have written more recently about altering the basis on which money is created is F.A. Hayek in his *Denationalisation of Money* (Institute of Economic Affairs, London, 1976). Hayek, however, was largely concerned with allowing competition between sources of money to allow users to choose those which held their value best in times of inflation.
5. *Dictionary of the English Language,* Collins, London, 1979.
6. P. Ormerod, *Butterfly Economics,* Faber, London, 1998, p.vii.
7. D. Begg, S. Fischer, R. Dornbusch, *Economics,* 5th Edition, McGraw-Hill, Maidenhead, 1997, p.375.

8. V. Morgan, *A History of Money*, Penguin, Harmondsworth, 1965, p.23.
9. 'Monetary Policy in the United Kingdom', Bank of England factsheet, August 1998.
10. J. K. Galbraith, *Money: Whence it came, where it went.* Penguin, Harmondsworth, 1976, p.29.
11. H. E. Daly, *Steady State Economics*, Earthscan, London, 1992, p.118.
12. H. E. Daly, 'Sustainable Growth: An Impossibility Theorem', in *Valuing the Earth: Economics, Ecology, Ethics*, H. E. Daly and K. N. Townsend, MIT Press, Cambridge, Mass., 1993.
13. C. Clark, 'The Economics of Over-Exploitation', *Science*, 181, pp.630-4, 1973.
14. H. Brodie, *Inishkillane: Change and Decline in the West of Ireland*, Penguin Books, Harmondsworth, 1974.
15. G. Davies, *A History of Money*, University of Wales Press, Cardiff, 1994.
16. L. Klingman and G. Green, *His Majesty O'Keefe*, London, 1952.
17. J. K. Galbraith, *Money: Whence it came, where it went.* Penguin, Harmondsworth, 1976, p.29.
18. *50 Ans Cercle Economique WIR*, WIR Basle, 1984.
19. See R. Douthwaite, *Short Circuit*, Green Books, Totnes, 1996, pp.107-8 for more details. See also Ralph Borsodi's *Inflation and the Coming Keynesian Catastrophe*, 1989, available from the E.F. Schumacher Society (Box 76, RD3, Great Barrington, MA 01230, USA).
20. B. Lietaer, personal communication, 30 August 1999.
21. F. Schwartz, 'Sechs-Stunden-Tag im Mittelalter', which appeared in the book *Vorwärts zur felten kaufkraft des geldes und zur zinsfreien wirtschaft*, 1931.
22. Carlo M. Cipolla, *The Monetary Policy of 14th Century Florence*, University of California Press, Berkeley, 1982.
23. J. Robertson, *Monetary Policy and Fiscal Policy: The Question of Credit Creation*, circulated privately, August 1999.
24. A. Smith, *The Wealth of Nations*, Penguin, London, 1986.
25. P. Wilsher, *The Pound in your pocket*, Cassell, London, 1970.
26. M. Kennedy, *Interest- and Inflation-Free Money*, Permaculture Publications, Steyerberg, Germany, 1990.
27. Personal communication, September 1999.
28. Personal communication, September 1999.
29. Natural Resources Defense Council and others, *Kingpins of Carbon: How Fossil Fuel Producers Contribute to Global Warming*, New York, July 1999.
30. M. Deane and R. Pringle, R., *The Central Banks*, 1994, Viking Penguin, New York.
31. R. Douthwaite, *Short Circuit*, Green Books, Totnes, 1996, p.122-3.
32. *Inflation—Dormant, Dying or Dead?* Central Bank of Ireland Technical Paper No. 6/RT/94, 1994.
33. 'Monetary Policy in the 21st Century: An Impossible Task?' *The Cato Journal*, Vol. 17, No.3.

Resource Guide

If you wish to follow up the hyperlinks detailed below, go to Green Books' website at <http://www.greenbooks.co.uk/ecomoney.htm>, where this Resource Guide is reproduced.

History of money: J.K. Galbraith's *Money: Whence it came, where it went* (Penguin, various printings) is the best introduction, particularly as it is delightful to read. Glyn Davies' *A History of Money* (University of Wales Press, Cardiff, 1994) is more detailed and has a much wider scope. Roy Davies' website at <http://www.ex.ac.uk/~RDavies/arian/amser/chrono.html>, draws a lot of material from his father's book and is the site to visit first for information on most of the topics covered by the Briefing, especially because of its links to other sites.

New money systems generally: My book, *Short Circuit* (Green Books, Totnes, 1996) is still the best source. David Boyle's *Funny Money* (Harper Collins, London, 1999) covers seven US money systems, including Time Dollars and Ithaca Hours, in a highly readable, human-interest style. It is not, however, a practical guide. The best general website is <http://www.ex.ac.uk/~RDavies/arian/local.html> but also visit <http://www.transaction.net/money/>

LETS: Peter Lang's *LETS Work: Rebuilding the Local Economy* (Grover Books, Bristol, 1994) is a good practical guide to starting a system. Information can also be obtained from the two rival LETS promotional organizations in the UK. These are:

> LETSLINK UK, at 2 Kent Street, Portsmouth, PO1 3BS. Tel (44) 1705 730639, fax (44) 1705 730629, <http://www.letslinkuk.demon.co.uk/>

> LETSystems on the Michael Linton model: <http://www.gmlets.u-net.com/home.html#home>. No postal address is given.

In addition, look at LETStalk (<http://www.oneworld.org/lois>) for information about practical innovations and modifications. There is also an e-mail discussion list (econ-lets), which you can join by sending an e-mail to <mailbase@mailbase.ac.uk> with the message "join econ-lets", then add your name.

WIR: Write to WIR, Auberg 1, 4002, Basel, Switzerland. Tel (41) 61 277911. The Wirtschaftsring's own website is at <http://www.bancawir.ch>. French, German and Italian versions are available. An article on the system is available at <http://newciv.org/ncn/moneyteam.html>. Information about EU-funded experiments to replicate the WIR model in Ireland, Scotland, Amsterdam and Madrid can be found at <http://www.barataria.org/>. Much more detailed information about these experiments is available in a book I wrote with Dan Wagman, *Barataria: A Community Exchange Network for the Third System* (Aktie Strohalm, Utrecht, Netherlands, May, 1999). It is available from Aktie Strohalm, Oudegracht 42, 3511 AR Utrecht, price (postpaid) £10.

ROMA: Write to Gerry McGarry, Enterprise Connacht-Ulster, Clare Street, Ballyhaunis, Co. Mayo, Ireland, tel (353) 907 30170, fax 907 30679. Information is also available on the web at <http://www.barataria.org/> and in the Barataria book mentioned under WIR.

Time Dollars: Enough detailed information to start a Time Dollar system is given in a leaflet, 'The Time Dollar' by Edgar Cahn, available for $2 plus a self-addressed 110mm x 220mm envelope from Time Dollar, P.O. Box 19405, Washington DC 20036, USA. Existing Time Dollar systems are described in *Time Dollars* by Edgar Cahn and Jonathan Rowe (Rodale Press, Emmaus, Pennsylvania, 1992). The Time Dollar website is at <http://www.timedollar.org/>. Information about Time Dollars in England can be obtained from Fair Shares, City Works, Alfred Street, Gloucester, GL1 4DP. Tel (44) 1452 541 337.

Monetary Reform. Three recent books have snatched this topic from the realm of anti-semites and similar cranks and made it possible for reasonable people to discuss it again. Alan D. Armstrong's *To Restrain the Red Horse: The Urgent Need for Radical Economic Reform* (Towerhouse Publishing, 32 Kilbride Avenue, Dunoon, Argyll, PA23 7LH, Scotland, 1996, price £11.95) and Michael Rowbotham's *The Grip of Death: A study of modern money, debt slavery and destructive economics* (Jon Carpenter Publishing, 2 The Spendlove Centre, Charlbury, OX7 3PQ, England, £15) both provide excellent treatments of the problems created by issuing money on the basis of debt. Frances Hutchinson's *What Everyone Really Wants to Know about Money* (Jon Carpenter Publishing, 2 The Spendlove Centre, Charlbury, OX7 3PQ, England, £12) explains the errors in economic thinking which led to our money-system difficulties.

Two magazines in the field are well worth their subscription price. They are *The Social Crediter*, 16, Forth Street, Edinburgh EH1 3LH (£6 in UK, £9 overseas airmail) and *Sustainable Economics*, 12 Queens Road, Tunbridge Wells, Kent, TN4 9LU (£6 in UK, £8 overseas). The British Association for Monetary Reform has a website at <http://www.users.globalnet.co.uk/~bamr1/recomend.htm> with links to other sites.

The Global Commons Institute is run from 42, Windsor Road, London NW2 5DS, tel (44) 818 451 0778. Its website at <http://www.gci.org.uk> has links to other climate change sites.

THE SCHUMACHER SOCIETY
See the whole, make the connections,
identify appropriate scale

The Society builds on the legacy of economist and philosopher E. F. Schumacher, author of seminal books such as *Small is Beautiful*, *Good Work* and *A Guide for the Perplexed*. Guided by his intensely practical as well as spiritually informed vision, Schumacher wanted to give societies, communities and individuals appropriate tools for change. The Schumacher Society promotes human-scale solutions for an enhanced relationship between people and the environment.

At the heart of the Society's work are the Schumacher Lectures, held in Bristol every year since 1978, and now also in Liverpool and Manchester. At the lectures, distinguished speakers from all over the world discuss key aspects of the sustainable well-being of people living in harmony with the earth. Speakers have included Amory Lovins, Herman Daly, Petra Kelly, Jonathon Porritt, James Lovelock, Wangari Maathai, Matthew Fox, Sir James Goldsmith, Patrick Holden, George Monbiot, Maneka Gandhi, James Robertson and Vandana Shiva.

The main focus of the Society is educational work. Tangible expressions of our efforts over the last 20 years are: the Schumacher Lectures; Resurgence Magazine; Green Books publishing house; Schumacher College at Dartington, and the Small School at Hartland, Devon, a demonstration model of human-scale education.

The Society is based in Bristol and London. It is a non-profit making company limited by guarantee. We receive charitable donations through the Environmental Research Association based in Hartland, Devon.

Schumacher Society Members receive:

- a free lecture ticket for either Bristol, Liverpool or Manchester
- the Schumacher Newsletter
- the catalogue of the Schumacher Book Service
- information about Schumacher College Courses
- a list of other members in your area, on application

The Schumacher Society, The CREATE Centre, Smeaton Road, Bristol BS1 6XN Tel/fax: 0117 903 1081
<schumacher@gn.apc.org> <www.oneworld.org/schumachersoc>

SCHUMACHER BRIEFINGS

The Schumacher Society is now extending its outreach with the Schumacher Briefings—carefully researched, clearly written 20,000-word booklets on key aspects of sustainable development, to be published three times a year. They offer readers:

• background information and an overview of the issue concerned
• an understanding of the state of play in the UK and elsewhere
• best practice examples of relevance for the issue under discussion
• an overview of policy implications and implementation.

The first three Briefings are as follows:

No 1: Transforming Economic Life: A Millennial Challenge by James Robertson, published in co-operation with the New Economics Foundation. Chapters include Transforming the System; A Common Pattern; Sharing the Value of Common Resources; Money and Finance; and The Global Economy.

No 2: Creating Sustainable Cities by Herbert Girardet. Shows how cities can dramatically reduce their consumption of resources and energy, and at the same time greatly improve the quality of life of their citizens. Chapters include Urban Sustainability, Cities and their Ecological Footprint, The Metabolism of Cities, Prospects for Urban Farming, Smart Cities and Urban Best Practice.

No 3: The Ecology of Health by Robin Stott. This Briefing is concerned with how environmental conditions affect the state of our health; how through new processes of participation we can regain control of what affects our health, and the kinds of policies that are needed to ensure good health for ourselves and our families. *(To be published in December 99)*

Future Briefings will deal with issues such as education, food and farming, globalization, local development, environmental ethics, energy policy, alternatives to genetic engineering and green technology. The Briefings are being published by Green Books on behalf of the Schumacher Society. To take out a subscription, or for further details, please contact the Schumacher Society office (see page 79)